Theo John Nielsen
January 20, 1922 – November 27, 1997

Doris Elaine Thorup Nielsen
January 18, 1922 – January 9, 1996

A collection of thoughts, stories, experiences, poetry, philosophy, art and handiwork by Theo and Doris Nielsen

Thank you to all of the Children and Grandchildren who have allowed their poems, letters and pictures to be shared with all of us.

A special Thank you To Kiersten Nebeker for her talent in publishing and Jeffrey Evans for typing one of Grandpa's Stories.

As you read these poems, stories and thoughts of Dad's and Mom's, we hope you come not only to know them better, but that you feel of their love for us and for the Gospel of Jesus Christ.

They lived what they taught. Their Testimony is one of our most treasured possessions.

Doris Elaine Nielsen
Signature of applicant

Theo Nielsen
Signature of bishop/branch president

Preface

I have wondered about what I could leave your children to help them remember their grandparents. Pictures will keep the image in mind. A few paintings and a few poems will give insight as to the character of their progenitor. Recorded experiences will testify as to the goodness of our god to his children.

After some thought, I have decided that I have not altogether forgotten my grandchildren. I have left them a tutor - you. I spent years training you for the job. You know how I feel about this and that and would respond to situations according to your training in this life, and your training in your previous life.

I reached this conclusion after much thought about my own parents. I have no words from any of my parentage. No poem, no painting, no thoughts of any kind. In one way or another I was robbed of the tutelage that was rightfully mine. See to the tutelage you owe your children and my grandchildren and on through time generation after generation.

Maybe Lehi had a good idea about how to pass on the thoughts and experiences that mold a life. [Below: Theo and Elise Nielsen Vowels]

-Theo John Nielsen

Titles and First Lines

1. I Had a Dream
2. Birth
3. Time Has a Way
4. What do you do with 17?
5. Time Moves On
6. One Drab Day
7. Plant a Seed
8. Changing of the Guard
9. A Letter from Doris to her Family
10. As a Sub-Teenager
11. How do you Describe a Person's Worth
12. Dear Shell-Pie
13. Adam
14. A Peek Into Hell
15. Doris' journal entries
16. How to Make a Man
17. The Little Frog in a Big Whirlpool
18. God – Christ
19. A Sacred Obligation
20. The Way it was, How it feels to be a Hero.
21. Understanding comes from Experience
22. Your Beauty is Beyond Description
23. Reason Tells Me Something's Wrong
24. In Creative Things Begun
25. Did You Ever Think That You would See
26. I Search for High Adventure
27. Recipe for Discouragement
28. I have a Son
29. Utilizing Time Properly
30. Dear Wendy – (Dad Tells about Mom)
31. Truth
32. If I Get Married, I'd Like it to Last
33. Life in Animas
34. Blessings our Family Has Received from Genealogy and Temple Work
35. Egbert's
36. For Doris
37. I Have a Message I'd Like to Pass

38. 50 Years
39. Entitlement Awards Earned During World War II for Theo John Nielsen
40. Dear Terri and Wendy – (Dating and Marriage Advise)
41. When I Was a Boy (Impressions of Grief at a Funeral)
42. Some Things are of This World
43. The Source of the Greatest Joy in this Life
44. News and Media
45. Only the Names Have Been Changed to Protect the Guilty
46. Guide to the Scriptures
47. Our Family Unit
48. Dear Good Buddy (TJ) – (Home in Idaho)
49. Christ
50. My Reward
51. Lack of Talent
52. Dear John
53. Maturity
54. Reflections of a Mother of 13
55. Intolerant Intolerance
56. Sparkle and Bubble
57. Poem to Jay
58. Mission
59. Forgiven
60. How did it Happen?
61. Parenthood
62. How Often Are we Led Astray
63. The Years Have Come and Gone Their Way
64. Leadership
65. Flesh of My Flesh
66. O Love, You Illusive Thing
67. Life
68. Teach My Child
69. Dreams
70. The Gods
71. My Youth
72. Integrity
73. Time is a Sometimes Thing
74. If I Could Walk Back in History
75. What is a Hankie
76. Love

77. Priesthood Song
78. The Sleeping Sitter
79. 1971 Spiritual Experience – Doris
80. My Day at the Branch Library – Doris
81. Our Trip to Disneyland – Doris
82. March 7, 1948, Elaine' Birth – Doris
83. May 2, 1962, Ty's Birth - Doris
84. 1993 Year End Summary - Doris
85. Dear Family - Doris
86. Dec. 17, 1982 - Doris
87. A Brief History of Their Courtship - Theo
88. Christ Like Life
89. A Computer Techs Song
90. Tradition
91. History
92. Buster
93. Dusty 1 – The Dogs Perspective
94. Dusty II – The Dog
95. Lost

(1)   I Had a Dream

I dreamt of faraway places, adventure, riches and fame.
I pictured myself in the center of life's stages. In all things I did excel.

While these dreams were vapor in my head, the inevitable was taking place. Time was marching through my life relentlessly.

I am well aware that the position in center stage requires prerequisites. While time was marching, the pressures of life pushed the training, the practices, and the urgencies into the background; then one by one the ambitions were laid aside until all my early thoughts and hopes were and never will be more than that- vapor that long ago was.

What compelling pressures could thwart the ambitions?
The first unscheduled intervention was a war that took me into circumstances that precluded the pursuit of personal ambitions.

The war was not yet finished when another and equally urgent desire came to the fore.

I recognized the girl I believe God made for me. After I had persuaded her to be mine, and the war had closed, happiness and responsibility multiplied with the relentless march of time. One by one the desires earlier treasured were rationalized away as they no longer were possible for one reason or another.

It was not that I was being cheated by some person or circumstance, it was that as situations changed I made choices that were to sort the important accomplishments from the selfish. At length the time was gone, the health was insufficient and the time that remained was needed for those things that were of greatest importance.

There were times when old dreams came to mind and the treasured thrills were felt in the imagination.

These thrills were only fleeting and reality soon took its rightful place. A wistful smile the only remaining evidence of an all but forgotten dream.

I have a dream. Now the dream includes others. Those of my loved ones who can share my dream. A dream that has no termination. All other dreams have had.

My dream can and will be realized. We are well on the road to that goal and with proper diligence will realize the greatest of all dreams. Life Eternal in the company of each other and with those we most admire.

Our eternal gratitude and love for our God, the Father, our brother, God the Christ, and all those through the ages who have served our needs, making possible the hope we now share.

I know we will be blessed and sustained in our efforts to obtain our hope. I now know that all blessings are a result of obedience to the law which governs that particular blessing. One cannot exist without the other.

-Theo John Nielsen

(2) [Birth]

Birth
Breath
Wiggle
Walk
Bubble
Babble
Tumble
Talk
Love
Live
Take
Give
Grow
Beau
Prom
Tom
Wed
Ned

(3) Time Has A Way

Time has a way of letting us build
Time has a way of showing what's gild
Time has a way of letting us know
What's for real and what's for show.

In my time I want to discover
Eternal laws – Make them my cover.
My armor, and my compass as well
And maybe avoid – Eternal hell.

(4) What Do You Do With 17?

What do you do with seventeen?
When the world is discovered again
What do you do with eighteen?
And life is beyond your kin
What do you do with nineteen?
When everything's so sure
What do you do with twenty?
When everything's still pure
And then we come to twenty one
When life has passed you by

(5) Time Moves On

Time moves on, we mellow, grow
The bigots' sight more dim
Summers sun andwinters snow
Bring thoughts closer to Him.

(6) One drab day

One drab day adds to another
Days and weeks add into years
There is no use to try
Then one day it's a whole new world
The sun comes up again
For you see from obscurity
Appears the kid next door
The tangled hair, the tattered clothes
Aren't there anymore.

(7) Plant a Seed

Plant a seed, watch it grow,
Train it in the way to go.
First to bloom, then to flourish
Carefully tend, not to perish.

In my garden there are many
Rich am I, not by penny.
But with the wealth of long untold
Never measured by mere gold.

In my garden children grow
Running, turning to and fro.
Antics by the bushel seen,
Little ones must please the Queen.

Their antics are achievements now
Some have bled, none will bow.
Varied tho' their goals may seem,
Each one aids the Father's Dream.

-Theo John Nielsen

(8) Changing of the Guard

In history, we find people who have special or extraordinary talent in special fields. Music composition at a very young age. Some of the sciences have had people who have excelled in learning. They have had a tremendous passion for a particular subject. How do people embrace these subjects with such adore? I don't think I have ever felt the urge to sacrifice any or all to succeed in any particular subject.

There is one thing that might be construed as a passion for accomplishment. I have always had a desire to see my family united in all their important aspects. Not in their work, or play, but in unity, loyalty, a solid front. No jockeying for position. No political stresses, but saturated with tolerance and forgiveness. It is scary to realize that you are about to pass to another world leaving your work incomplete.

Have I effectively instilled the proper principles to leave a united posterity?

Do we have enough passion for unity to survive the changing of the guard?

TJ Nielsen

(9) A letter from Doris Elaine Thorup Nielsen to her family
11/10/1991 Sunday 11:00am, Just prior to Heart Surgery

"I want to tell them all how much I love them. I'm grateful for your families. But I want them to know to live the gospel no matter what. Then you can have peace. It isn't that hard if you follow the teachings. Live the law of the land where ever you are. You may not always agree with them, but they don't interfere with your life. It's like obeying the traffic laws when you're driving. If you run a red light you will pay the consequences. If you don't live moral laws, it's the same as the laws of the land. You may not think that you're hurting anyone or that anyone will know, but they do.

Tell the Grandkids that I love them. They have good parents, obey them. As long as you're obedient, you'll never be sorry.

I love you,

Grandma

(10) As a sub-teenager

As a sub-teenager I attended a stake conference. President Grant was present and spoke. I was so moved that wonderful thoughts came into my head, and I almost had to wonder why I was not called up to the podium to express these profound ideas. Today, of course, I have no idea what they were, but I do know that I was moved. You see, I can relate to your experience.

Your article is well written, and makes me proud of your ability to express yourself. Now I have a request of you. In five or ten years read your offering again and determine if there are any changes, or additions you'd like to make.

Dad   [Sent to Terri as a fax 1997]

(11) How do you describe a person's Worth?

How do you describe a person's worth?
Some people say she is down to earth
Others say she is a lamb, a jewel.
Shallow comments from a thoughtless pool.

Then, whenever I bask in her smiles,
Her acts of love and her extra miles,
I think of more than a pretty face
I think of the things born of inner grace.

Her mother's life, lived in loving deeds
By serving others and those in need.
With real concern she's living the same-
Her mother's pattern deep in her grain.

So then live in cheer with no regret.
Life was not meant for remorse and sweat.
Life was meant to be lived in high gear-
Robust, vigorous, full of good cheer.

When this life is o'er, run its course,
When judged by Him who may indorse
Familiar voices to resound
Great shall be the joy that abounds.

TJ Nielsen

(12) Dear Shell-Pie,

I owe you several letters, so here they are. I could tell you that it rained last night, but what difference does it make? One of the cows had twins, so what? What I would like to leave you is something you can use today, tomorrow, always.

The most important thing in this life or any other life is love. The most important act in your life will be a proper marriage. Do you know why people divorce? Their marriage has gone stale. They read books that portray the joy of fresh, new love. Theirs is so drab. The movies also motivate us to a desire for new, fresh love.

What happened to the fresh new love we once had? We let it tarnish, fade, rust, mold, diminish. When I was young I planned a fishing trip at 4:00am. At 3:30 am my new wife woke me, breakfast was ready. When I opened my lunch there was a note inside for my eyes only. On ordinary days I would find notes in my lunch. When I was working out of town I would find notes in my pockets when I put on my clean, fresh clothing my wife packed for the trip.

She continuously scrubbed our marriage trying always to keep it bright, and shiny. At home, at church, at play at work. She would find a way to make me look good. Even when we were alone she would manufacture a situation where my ego would be enhanced.

She never tried to make me over. She coached me in a subtle way that I might acquire social grace. I could ask what to do in a given situation, and I would be helped without embarrassment.

This should give you an idea of the things I wanted to tell. I love you.

Puppy   [Shell-pie is Michele Crane Farr, she called Grandpa "Puppy"]

(13)   Adam

When Adam was placed in the Garden of Eden, he was given a problem to solve. Why should he give up all this easy living He finally decided to take the plunge? By the sweat of his brow, against the weeds, clay dirt, and hot sun. Have you ever noticed when one problem is solved there is a new problem to take its place?

Research and science have conquered one disease after another but there is always another new malady to take the place of the old.

In our personal lives the pattern is the same. Why is the great hulk of a body furnished with a tender sensitive heart?

Which is dominant, the tender heart or the massive body?

The scriptures say the spirit should dominate the body. Mind over matter. How far and how fast must a man change? If it is possible.

We need the reason and the will to change the pattern of our lives. Conviction and satisfaction are the rewards for true mental orientation.

Why is one given a little less body and a little more heart? Why is the way made easier for some and harder for others? Where is the equality? Why should one have his path made smooth, no ruts, or rocks no financial problems, no marital or social difficulties. Could it be that the challenges facing one are not the same as those confronting another?

Is it a fact that some are born to easier lives?

The fact is each of us has our own life to live, not to compare, except with ourselves.

If I am the record holder for the sprint with no competition, I race against the clock. Can I exceed the old record? The only fair comparison is myself.

Your Dad

(14) A Peek Into Hell

I peeked into hell today,
Things seemed to be serene.
I peeked into hell today,
So pretty lush and green.

Gay colors worn everywhere,
Happiness filled the scene.
Humor and goodwill were there,
Tranquil and peaceful it seemed.

I was puzzled and confused,
Another look inside might help.
No one there seemed abused,
What was so dreadful? Tell.

Confused by conflicting thoughts,
I took the time to think
What you see is what you're taught,
And then my heart did sink.

It wasn't what I thought I saw,
It's what I felt that mattered
In spite of the pictures they draw,
All their hopes were shattered.

And yet they live on pretending,
Goals always short of real
Thoughts, like backs ever bending,
Never able to break their seal.

TJN

(15) [Journal entry - Doris Elaine Thorup Nielsen 9/11/1984]

It was sure a change and fun to go with the girls.   Wish I could just sit and enjoy with my hip and leg pain.

Fall is upon us. The leaves are starting to turn.

Lying on my bed this morning making plans for the day
I suddenly realized – My pains had gone away –
And as I lay there thinking, I was quick to decide
I had forgotten the "simple" joys of being alive.

To plan, to wash, to clean, to bake some bread.
To curl hair, to wash faces, iron a shirt or make a bed
My responsibilities are somewhat changed as the children have grown and gone.
But the joys of a new day should still be strong.

Song in my heart, quilt on the frame,
Fruit in the jars – why should anyone complain.
A loving husband beside me – children you love and adore.
Bringing their precious young to visit – Now can one ask for more?

Parents and family have taught me who I am.
Acknowledge of Christ's love, and His Fathers plan.

I pray I can remember the blessings I enjoy.
And use my time wisely, as each morning appears.
Remembering my Fathers goodness to His children who obey
Learn to do what's right in every single way.

Help me remember as my pains come back again
My blessings are so numerous I should never complain.

(16) How to make a man

I believe the first step in the development of a man is to convince the boy, at an early age, he will become a man. If he doesn't believe he can be a man, he never will be one.

An experience: A three-year-old boy was sent out to feed the milk cow. He put on his boots, heavy coat, stocking hat and gloves. With a smile on his face he went out the back door. His mother was waiting for the father to go help, but he made no move. Aghast she exclaimed, "Honey!"

When the boy reached the hay stack, there were no broken bales. I'm not sure how much the boy weighed, but maybe half the weight of a bale of hay. After a minutes hesitation the boy walked out of sight. You may imagine the conversation taking place behind the kitchen window.

The boy came back into sight, pulling his sled. He pulled the sled as close to the bale of hay as possible, and with great effort, rolled the hay a quarter turn onto the sled. With this maneuver he was able to get the hay next to the feeder. Problem number one solved, he began to tackle the next: How to break the bale and get it into the feeder. The next thing he did was produce an axe. He had seen his brother cut the wires on the bales, so this took no imagination. The one thing it did take was strength enough to cut the wire. He flayed those wires with all his might, and it began to look like dad was going to be forced to assist. Of a sudden one wire broke making a crescent of the bale. With head held high, the lad gave about half of a bale of hay to the anxious cow. When the boy came back into the house his face was a picture of triumph. You may have supposed he had just been elected President of the United States.

Yes, he expected more from the boy than he was capable, but if that is not the case, if we expect less than a boy is capable, that's exactly what we will get.

Before this year is over, I will have ninety-four descendants or those espoused to my descendants. It is a little difficult to write to each and every one of these on a person basis. It has always been a chore for me to write a check let alone a letter, so, having a desire to promote the good life for my children, I have decided to write a letter to one and all that would encompass all the things that might make you happy for eternity.

(17) The Little Frog in the big pool

I have written and rehearsed tales of how our Father in Heaven has interfered in my life to preserve same. There are at least half a dozen of these experiences that I know about. There are probably more of which I'm not aware.

It has always been my desire to be morally clean, of these incidents where I have been helped to maintain my virtue I've been more reserved. Some of the circumstances were scary, and some were comical.

As the years and generation pass these experiences will fade into tradition or rambles of a senile old man. I pray these may be counted as few, that the more part of my descendants will have the vision of eternity to use as a help.

I have always known there is a God our Father. There were times when I doubted the worth of time expended on me. "The little frog in the big pool."

(18) God Christ

I just wanted to assure you that God and Christ still live and are enjoying good health.

When I think about some of the things they have done for me it becomes mind-boggling. Imagine the love necessary to prompt such a sacrifice as Jesus made.

(19) A Sacred Obligation

Persons of influence have a sacred obligation to use that influence for good. Be they famous for singing, dancing, political or religious affiliation. These people, the latter, more than any other should be humble and prayerful about the things they say or do.

Some Celebrities, a good example of a poor example, has been raving for twenty –five years about things they have insufficient knowledge. It's a shame they have the time and money to spread their misinformation.

A few days ago the T.V. had an article about a man who has spent his life down-grading the morals of people. He said there is no God, there should be no prayer in schools, you are obligated to promote yourself, do your own thing, free sex. He is an old man now and wiser. He is going through his records and trying to correct the errors he made. He is writing to former students to tell them he was in error: there is a God. All the things God has recommended for happiness in this live is true. He purchased time on T.V. in an attempt to reach former students and correct his teachings. Think of the sorrow he caused in the fifty--odd years he spent in rebellion. A good many teachers feel the need to expound on subjects of which they have no knowledge.

While working at the U of U, I heard a number of the professors preaching anti-god instead of the subject assigned.

(20) The Way it was.

How it feels to be a hero.

Somewhere in the So. Pacific during World War II about 6 pm. some enemy aircraft were making a run on us to launch their torpedoes.

They launched, we heeled over and came about at 90 degrees to course. We were missed.

The Cambara was on our port quarter but not so lucky. They were struck in the engine room and left dead in the water.

Another heavy cruiser took her in tow at two knots.

We were within range of the enemy's land based planes. They were determined to make the most of their advantage.

The next day about the same time, the same set of circumstances existed. The exception to this was that the doomed ship was the Houston.

The performances were duplicated of the day before. The Houston was taken in tow by two destroyers. Their speed was again two knots.

The main part of our fleet left as a part of our strategy. There were several hundred miles between the crippled ships and the fleet.

We were elected to remain behind and protect the crippled ships. They, and we, were considered expendable. It was hoped the enemy would come out for the kill. Our fleet would then come back and hopefully destroy the enemy.

From the point where we were it would take five days for the disabled ships to be out of range of the enemy land based planes.

During that five days the enemy would spare no effort in trying to sink the two stricken ships with their sparse escort.

Those bent on our destruction seemed to have an uncanny sense of timing. If we tried to eat at 5 pm., they were there. If we tried to eat at 4 pm they were there.

Moving at two knots the "expendables", or "bait" would be several days moving far enough away from the land based planes to be out of danger. It was hoped that in those several days, the Japanese fleet would come out of hiding and try to finish the small group of ships.

If this should happen, the main fleet would be within striking distance and with any luck, finish the remaining ships of the Japanese fleet.

During the next five days, the land based planes were very active, but the Japanese fleet never came out to do battle.

There was no sleep for anyone, because the strikes from the Japanese land based planes went around the clock. Those ships that were not crippled were going in a circle around the towed ships at a speed of twenty-seven knots.

After five days the distance was enough to give relief enough for a meal and the galley was opened without interruption. It was a welcome relief from the tension.

Speaking of tension, I'll have to tell you about the third or maybe the fourth night. We were sitting around our CQ station. Some were playing cards, some listening to the radio, others just talking. Everyone was on edge. The door opened and Felstein came in dressed in a grass skirt and all the trimmings. He grinned, did a couple of taps with his right foot, and got our attention, and then started into a "do as you go" routine that was vigorous if not talented. He slowed down, we clapped our hands, whistled, stomped our feet. The appreciation gave Felstein the motivation to put all he had into his show. He danced until he was covered with sweat and couldn't pick up his feet. This may not have been the greatest act in the world, but there could have been none better for us at that time.

The war went on, we joined the fleet. One day we were told the fleet was going to drop anchor at Ulithi, an atoll that made a good harbor, in the middle of nowhere. We were the last ship to enter the harbor. The reason became obvious as we passed the other ships already anchored.

As we came down the channel we came abreast the Cambarra and as capital ships do there was a formal salute. All hands on deck, at attention facing the other ship. At the command of the bugle all hands on board salute the other ship.
The captain of the Cambarra read a tribute, then all their crew gave three cheers and threw their hats in the air.

We moved on past the Houston and they did the same thing.

I really felt worthwhile that day.

-Theo John Nielsen
World War II Veteran

(21) Understanding Comes from Experience

If you have never tasted a particular fruit or vegetable can you say you like it, or dislike it?

From time to time, over the years, my wife has had the excuse that her nerves would bother her. After some twenty years of hearing this fake excuse, I privately scoffed. Suddenly I was shocked by a feeling never known before. The feeling lasted only an instant, but it shook me to the core: That was of another's malady.

On another occasion I was called to the stand the judge asked if I was on any medication that would affect my testimony. I replied that I was fine.

During the course of my interrogation I became aware of counsel repeating a question over and over again. I answered each time but it became apparent he was playing with my mind I didn't know just how, but I was being discredited as a witness. I had with me a document covering the question. I handed the document to the attorney telling him that his answer was before him in writing. The medication was affecting me even though I could not tell how.

Understanding comes from experience.

Since that time my experience has taught me that medication can effect your perception; pain can do the same. Emotions, stress, conditioning, past experience, or inexperience, can do the same. It is difficult to know when all you have to judge from is your own frame of reference.

One more experience, with a sequel, and I believe I will have made my point.

On August 17, 1945 aboard the carrier Wasp, the following occurred:

Our newest fighter planes were returning from a mission. One plane came in unexpectedly quick. The time gap between the two planes was too short. I looked up from my note pad to see the position of the next plant to land, and all I could see was the cowling. The plane was out of control, had missed the cable with its hook, and was headed for the parked planes forward. I was between the runaway and the tile parking areas. As I turned to run, I was struck violently in the back, causing me to move forward into the elevator of the plane that had just been parked. The double shock upset me causing me to loose my footing and I was on my face, flat on the deck. I knew it was too late to get up and run, so I decided to roll. One half turn and I was against the tail wheel of the last parked plane.

Realizing I was as good as dead, I was overcome with a feeling of peace. I relaxed, and calmly, and very sincerely, said to my intended, "Good-bye, honey."

I was in that state watching the propeller spin, and coming to a stop, when I was again the irate offended. I jumped to my feet and was looking for the man next to be punished for upsetting me. Eight men came running to me, one exclaimed, "I saw it!" I asked "What was it?" All eight said I was alone. I pressed them for a name with no result.

When I had time to calm myself, and ponder the experience I was forced to the conclusion that once again my Father in Heaven had intervened in my life, and I had been spared.

Time and events passed, and I became a grandfather. My sixth girl became a mother. Her daughter was four or five years of age when her mother decided to tell her of her carrier experience of her grandfather. At the conclusion of the story the child said "I remember that, that's when we pushed grandpa down."

[Nancy and Bryan were watching "Tora, Tora, Tora" A World War II film and on it there was an air craft carrier. Nancy began to tell the above story. Then Nova said, "That is when we pushed grandpa down."]

(22) Your Beauty Is Beyond Description

Your beauty is beyond description
 Your movements personifying grace
Whenever you're near life's sure to be fun
No, wonder, as I look in your face

We've been wed now, a year, maybe more.
Yesterday's dishes still in the sink
Yesterday's clothes strewn round the floor
Dinner is late, five minutes I think.

Dad

(23) Reason Tells Me

Reason tells me something's wrong
My exaltation for a song?
Why did the Savior suffer so?
Just to show the way to go?
Did he plan the Father to please?
That we might ascend with such ease?
Or is there more that we should do?
"There is a law – "Will give a clue
If I may have all that is his.

(24) In creative things began

In creative things began
Not at all the common run
But things that build, things of hope
With no bounds nor tied by rope

To think, build or work a plan
Go alone or with a clan
To create, to make your own
Build a book or carve in stone.

(25) Did you ever think that you would see…

Did you ever think that you would see
One filled with so much talent as me
One who creates with such a flourish?
Words of wisdom never to perish
Rich is the man who from them can glean
And add wealth and comfort to life's scheme.
The possibilities have no end
And the welfare you a check will send.

(26) I search for high adventure

I search for high adventure
The blood rushes in my veins
To alter a champions venture
To conquer desert and plains

But now I'm getting older
My blood doesn't run as fast
Winter is so much colder
All the fire of youth is past

I've seen life from front and back
And say with authority sure
To know self, this is a fact
Crowns the highest adventure

(27) Recipe for Discouragement

Into any amount of good works add 1 oz. of jealousy. Any brand may be used. Stir gently as vigorous work will not allow ingredients to ferment. If mishandled properly, this is one of the speediest forms of discouragement.

This is only a sample recipe. If you would like our free booklet, do nothing.

(28) I Have a Son

I have a son – tall and strong
He's been gone – not too long;
Of late his live has been a whirl
Run, turn no, no, that's a girl.

Pressures and excitement fade
Now he's left to pull the grade
Now there's time to look around
Just how in this world he's found.

"Oh it's great to be on my own,
My little faults don't bring a groan"
I come and go as I please
Hold it fella, at ease.

What a Mob, push and shove
You'd think they'd show me some love
Why do they irritate me so?
Is there no other way to go?

Yet for me it's not so bad
Elaine's the one that really sad!

(29) Utilizing Time Properly

I suppose there is a lot to be said for the advantages of utilizing time properly. Usually this is interpreted as "don't waste time" which is interpreted as "hurry." My interpretation of "hurry" is "hit the high spots."

"Accomplishing something" with your time had to do with "things" - things material. Life has its "ups" and its "downs." If we hurry, we are able to feel the highs and maybe glance into the hollows.

If we only "hit" the highs we are unable to descend the slopes, walk through the valleys or climb the rise on the other side. Each valley is a new experience. A new growth

There are, of course, places we do not go, things we do not experience.

If we see a glowing piece of metal and feel its radiating heat, we do not put our hand on the hot metal to confirm the finding of our other senses.

There are evils all around us that we are aware of, but we know better than to partake of these things.

(30) Dear Wendy,

Because you are the youngest you knew Mom the shortest time. On the other hand, you were with her the longest alone. Regardless, I want to tell someone about her special beauty, and I elected you.

We had in South Jordan a nice looking lady with a homely daughter. The mother wore glasses, not the daughter. On one occasion I called at their home when there were no specs worn. The artist in me compared features finding them quite similar. The experience prompted me to analyze the difference in appearance.

When I reached home I recounted the happening to your Mother. At first she thought it had something to do with the glasses. We discussed the matter for a time and came to the conclusion that the lady was an outstanding example of inner beauty. The story has a happy ending, as time and maturity etched into the daughter's life she became markedly the likeness of her mother.

Your mother had no such problem. As you can see from photographs she was beautiful from the first.

In the third grade, she was passing with some girl friends, and I looked up from the dirt and offered her my prettiest marble. She refused same with barely a nod. In the fourth grade she offered aid and comfort to this wounded gladiator. She never had to learn compassion, it was part of her character.

As a teenager she taught mutual, and Sunday-school. Her character was apparent, and those in charge wanted to take the greatest advantage. Of course, with maturity her virtues expanded. In time her wrinkles betrayed her. They indicated the love she had especially for the down-hearted, the sad, the lonely, the abused, anyone needing empathy for any reason.

She was serious, she was humorous, she was thoughtful, she was joyful, and all the attributes in between. Was she perfect? Not quite, she would beat me at any game she could, as often as she could.

You may believe it when I tell you she is the most nearly perfect person I have ever known. I say this after fifty years of life with her, and ten years of dating, and letters and five years of school prior to that. That is about sixty-five years.

If anyone ever should say a word against her actions, or intentions, don't have any dealing with them.

Love ya,

Dad

(31) Truth

Why would a child of mine come to me, after being married long enough to have a large family, for reassurance of the truth I taught her many years ago? The answer to the question is: truth is being assaulted as never before.

Napoleon must have had the same problems. He said if a truth is a truth, is a truth, it must be truth forever. (Paraphrased.)

People suppose that a Prophet has the prerogative of change. This is not the case. A prophet must deal in truths. If he does not, he is not a Prophet. A prophet may emphasis a truth, he may initiate a program, he may speak out on current events, but he cannot reverse truth.

Our Father in Heaven is bound by truth, and always will be. Otherwise he will cease to be God.

Sex immorality (Mormon Doctrine Page 708)

Virtue may be lost by degrees; and chastity may be destroyed a step at a time. Immodesty, necking and petting, themselves a form of sex, immorality, frequently lead to much grosser offenses. Every degree and type are among Lucifer's chief means of leading souls to hell. Fine distinctions between them are of no particular moment and are not necessary to observance of the divine laws involved. Counsel in the field of chastity is simply: Be Chaste!

Truth is absolute and eternal; it endureth forever. (D and C 1:39; 88:66) It never varies; what is true in one age is true in every age. The theories of men (scientific or otherwise) vary from discovery to discovery and are in a continuing state of flux, unless they chance on a particular point to reach ultimate truth. Then there is no more change, and the truth discovered is in complete harmony with every other truth in every other field. Truth never conflicts with truth.

Wisdom of the World (Mormon Doctrine page 839)

The wisdom of the world is transitory; it will vanish away. But the wisdom of God is eternal; it will endure forever. Scientific theories change with every new discovery, but the wisdom revealed from God is eternal truth.

(32) Marriage

If I get married, I'd like it to last
Not just fun and over fast.
A Marriage should grow and bloom forever
Nothing less will do, never.

So we got married and grew and blossomed
I teased, at times too often.
I still tease a little, its attention
She returns love, it's mentioned

I tell the children for three generations
How we've lived, what our mission.
The love we've shared and sometimes the tears
A lot of joy, now and then fears.

Life moves on, it is thrill after thrill
The years ripen, as years will.
And the blossoms are richer than before
Instead of tease, I love you more.

When time's gone and life has seeped away
The flesh has won, it's had sway
Then you sit alone and live the past
Wondering how long time can last.

Someday when we've settled down forever
Building our hopes not to sever
Promises made by a loving Creator
Sharing all, not spectator.

T.J. Nielsen '96

(33) Life in Animas

Four weeks have passed, three here and one home one here. Every week there are about four men going and four coming from all over the United States. Most of the men are married but have forgotten. I have decided I have been leading a very sheltered life.

The reason for my being here is a new smelter, built in the middle of thousands of acres. We are starting the smelter into production.

After work I color on Kathleen's Centennial posters, it's going slow. Today is Sunday April 25th.

4/26/1976
Just got back to the trailer from the phone where I learned the busy regiment. Before that we were to another trailer where the fellow fixed pizza for Dick and I and my roommate who came along.

Now I'm in my room while Bob (that's the other inhabitant of this trailer) is watching TV.

I thought I'd put in writing a thought of this morning.

When no. 1 son was 15 years old I spoke to my wife, saying "Honey! Do you realize our boy is 15 years old and we have done absolutely nothing toward planning his mission?"

She agreed and we continued to religiously procrastinate.

In what seemed to be a few weeks I said, "Honey, do you know our boy is 17 years old and his mission is at the door and we are not ready yet."

Nearly two years slipped by the next short period and our boy would be 19 years old in the next few months and <u>I was not ready yet.</u> It was time for a crash program.

You know what a crash program is. That's when you do the best you can with what you have and when you're done your friends think your wife did it.

The only way I can see to finance his mission is to sell the home, build another with the equity and be free from debt.

It should be obvious to you who have had missionaries that at this point in time I knew nothing about He who supervises missionary work in the earth.

I intended to accomplish all this missionary support by myself.

5/1/1976

I unfold a clean shirt packed with tender care for the trip to Hidalgo- (Animas) New Mexico. It's the third shirt with a note in the pocket. My wife has found another way to remind me she loves me.

She's ahead of me in every way in thoughtfulness. I've found notes in sandwiches shirt pockets, sox – where and when least expected. What a doll!

(34) Blessings our family has received from Genealogy and Temple Work

This assignment is on a personal basis so … your charity will have to be on its best behavior.

At age 14, for some reason I don't now remember, I participated in a genealogy class and built my first book of remembrance.

It was at the time, that I came to understand that life was really endless and that my ancestors were in some place waiting for the keys in order to progress.

I came to understand that their work was a family affair. In doing research I came to know and admire my family. Even though I had never met them face to face these people became real. Those who have searched out their ancestors know what I mean. Those who have not, do not.

As I grew older and began to travel, this knowledge plus the knowledge of the requirements for entrance into the temple were a strength to me. The desire to commit the sins that would keep me from the Temple were never presented to me. I was greatly blessed.

At age 23 I married a girl who had been in that same genealogy class some nine years before. After marriage she told me that someone has asked her if she thought she would be married in the temple and she said "Of Course!"

They asked her if we had discussed the subject and she said NO!

We both knew the way for us to be married and there never was a discussion about it.

When the honeymoon was over and the trails of marriage became a reality I confess to the temptation of getting rid of an unreasonable wife. She did not always do it my way.

If my marriage had been a temporary marriage – for this life only- the temptation may have matured.

The eternity of marriage gives us the desire to do better and helps us to mature.

I have one son married in the temple. Two of my other children are engaged and express the desire for temple marriage. We also have several other teenagers at home. In preparation for this talk I asked them a few questions such as what if you are asked to marry outside of the Temple?

What has Genealogy and Temple Weddings done for you? Some of the response are.

- If he really wants me he'll want me forever.

- We feel a kinship we would not have otherwise.

- We, now, have the ability to research our kindred.

- If he can get a temple recommend I feel he has lived a better life.

The scriptures tell us we are to teach our children. The scriptures also tell us that if we fail to keep our promises made to the fathers, the whole earth will be utterly wasted at his coming.

I feel that our activity in genealogy and temple work are the best introduction we could give our children in this responsibility.

(35) Egberts

Sometimes we find a man who in times of stress comes through
Sometimes we find a wife who is loyal through and through
Sometimes we find a family bring their own up strong.
Sometimes we find a people who make us feel we belong
Some people love neighbors as Christ said, and are expert.
When all these things are found in one their name is EGBERT.

(36) For Doris

To let me know just what you think,
Write a poem of me said she
But if my thoughts are put in ink
You may wonder about me.

The years have passed and we have grown
More and More like each other.
O, how sweet life has flown
I would not trade another.

To say she is fair would be meager
She is so very much more
To extol her virtues I'm eager
In the use of words I'm poor

She's so soft, then hard as steel
She's generous to a fault
In every thought and act she's real
She is one that's worth her salt.

(37) I have a message I'd like to pass

I have a message I'd like to pass
How to say it is beyond my class
Struggle I must, for it will be said
Though some will say it's as good as dead

[This next paragraph was lightly crossed out]

Maybe it's the urge to do something good
To leave a "sign" or point a better way
It may guide a son some very sore day

I've struggled with the thoughts
They dance outside my reach
My brain is full of clots
I'm drained by some great leach

My paper full of starts
My pen can't seem to flow
My mind with rhythm pants
I've lost the way to go.

To turn, twist, struggle, toss
and yet appear so calm
An inner chasm to cross
Before I feel the balm

To pass my Treasure on
I must reveal myself,
The balance I'd freely pawn
Or credit to an Elf

And yet how could I know
The secret I would tell
If I had yet to go
The path I know so well

Torn by strife and anguish
Peace I had never known
Truth would always languish
I could but reach and groan

Torment driven here and there
Searching, yet not to find
Some say "Why should I care,
What is this peace of mind?"

Then when least suspected
There came within my being
Honor and respected
Thru' eyes of love seeing

She was and is beauty
Personified they say
And still she brought "duty"
Into my narrow day

No Longer free to go
When e'r the wave would toss
Hearing the winds that blow
And drive me till I'm cross

The habits of my youth
Seize and hold by my scarf
But I will swear in Truth
I long for love and hearth

I'm torn now as before
My treasure not yet found,

I could pass thru the door,
False pride upon the ground

I will not surrender
I am a man, you know
She's so small and tender
To love her I must grow

To grow in youth is easy
I know, now youth is gone
But build never ceasing
Working toward a dawn

The dawn when I'm stable
And know where I have been
To be strong and able
To face the foe or kin

To know and understand self
To accept me as I am
Choosing good from the pelf
Discard façade and sham.

(38) 50 Years

In fifty years of things I've done
More than all the things I've won
More than all the things I'm given
More than all my thoughts of Heaven

Turning sod or thought of man
Why follow another's plan?
Why measure the things of worth
With a yardstick born of earth

(Pictures Left: Doris 2 years old, Right: Theo 2 years old)

(39) Entitlement awards for Theo John Nielsen earned during World War II. (Service Number 660 44 47)

Branch of Service USNR

Dad lost his dog tags in the ocean. They broke off when he dove in for a swim.

Navy Good Conduct Medal   American Campaign Medal

Asiatic Pacific Campaign Medal with 1 Silver Star and 3 Bronze Stars

World War II Victory Medal   Navy Unit Commendation Ribbon Bar

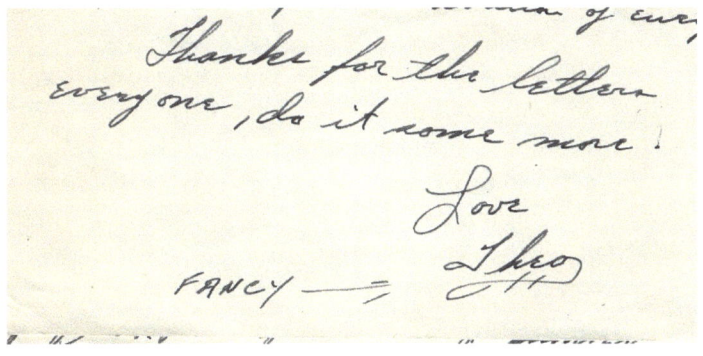

Foreign Awards

Philippine Liberation Ribbon with 2 Bronze Stars
Philippine Presidential Unit Citation

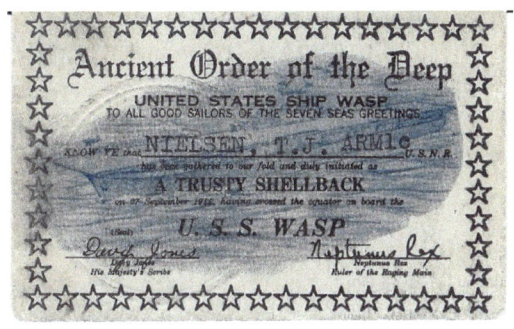

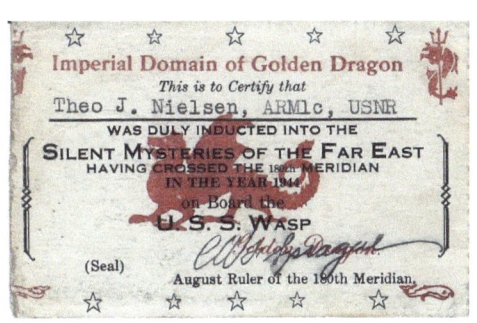

39

(40) Dear Terri and Wendy,

Parents have the desire to spare their children the hurts of any kind that may come their way. We try to teach a principle in an easy way – a soft approach. Unfortunately we sometimes miss making our point by being too soft. Fear of being in that category when the need is real, prompts this note.

It's time I told you about men. We are a cowardly thing. We have a great desire to serve ourselves. We enjoy others serving us. We enjoy our freedom. We avoid responsibility. The only time we will give up these things is if a greater desire pushes them aside.

That greater desire has to be urgent, demanding and overwhelming. We have to be willing to give up friends, face embarrassments or swallow pride. We must be strong enough to face the possibilities of being broke, driving an older car or being hurt! All of these possibilities will be ours at one time or another. Of course we can indulge ourselves in self pity. Self-pity is an excuse, not a reason. If a prior hurt is why we avoid a responsibility it would indicate too weak a character to face the vicissitudes of life. If that be the case a union with that person would end in divorce or servitude. Neither being a desirable situation.

When I asked your mother to marry me, all the reasons for not getting married disappeared. I wanted her near all the time – in my pocket if possible. I have no respect for a man who hides behind flimsy excuses, or selfish desires for justification in wrong doing.

A man who enjoys the advantages of the "singles" branch – companionship – "Dutch dates" or more, for an extended period is a poor excuse for manhood. In "Hazards of the Heart" the "creep" says "I will have her." If a man's honorable desire is not as powerful as the "creeps" don't give him another thought. He's lost in indecision and/or another of the discrediting weaknesses.

I love you,

Dad.

(41) When I Was a Boy

When I was a boy I was impressed by the grief shown by the family at a funeral and was struck by the idea that if you didn't care you wouldn't be hurt. This became my attitude to be developed over time. There are draw-backs in having this attitude, you become a "loner". You care for no one, and believe no one cares for you.

You can enjoy parties, dancing, sports, movies, but when they are over you "close the door" behind you.

This attitude can be nurtured if your parents are at odds with one another. Loyalty becomes impossible. It's easier to retreat to the "don't care" area where you need not fear the conflicts of others. The ultimate is to put them all out of your life, "close the door" socially, physically and geographically.

A teenager is too young to correct the errors of his surrounding, so he runs.

(What do you do when you are continually asked to take sides?)

Years of war, and living with other depressed persons help in the development of your "don't care" attitude.

At a visit, after the war, my mother asked me, "Why do you snap at me, why are you so hard?"

I had felt love at that time, but my love had a narrow focus, and short range. In fact, I had felt no real love.

Over the years with constant coaching from one who really knew, my years of "observer" practice faded, and I began to know joy. Today you might say "my cup runneth over." Fact is, I had to get a bigger cup.

My doctor tells me that there never has been a medication that didn't have side effects. About a hundred years ago an Englishman made a great discovery, he had identified the ancestor to the horse. A small skeleton, a few inches tall with five toes. Ideologies are like any other theories. When you have developed them into a conviction they have their side-effects.

I believe it would be counterproductive to relate the results further. We have no desire to provide supposed justification for any wrong-doing.

During the years of fantasy, I never lost my conviction of a God. A supreme being, one who created the earth, and all there is in it. I was sure I was the least of His concern. I never made any record of the number of interventions in my live that He made to preserve that life. With time they dim, and given enough time, the experiences fade into oblivion. I'll admit to the dimming but not to oblivion.

With proper coaching, and by committing some acts of love, you begin to see the side-effects surface on the other side of the ledger. My understanding has always lagged my years.

In the third grade marbles was my interest mud and all. One day while playing "pots" a few of the better dressed girls in my room were walking around the school. I'm not sure what prompted the boldness but as they passed I offered the one with the "glow" my finest "Bulls-eye". She ignored me, never breaking her stride. You couldn't blame her. I was mud to the knee. My hands were covered with clay, and I always needed a hair cut. A month or so later I was hurt. She wanted to know if there was anything she could do to help. Ten years later she agreed to be my coach.

(42) Some things are of this world

Some things are of this world, and others are of other times, and places. It is more important to have the knowledge that will enable us to cope with the present conflict than to know the mysteries of creation.

How does one build the will to resist evil when no one is watching? How do I learn the real value of service? Who is the greatest servant ever known? Why are only the best servants qualified for exaltation?

Ponder the mysteries, but do not devote you life to them. Spend your energy in the pursuit of truth, truths that will enhance your value to your kindred. Be energetic in your search for truth, and when you have found it, don't be an observer, be active in the spread and the embracing of the same.

The possessor of a mystery that has no current value has but one admirer, himself. The doer of a beneficial service has as many admirers as have a knowledge of his service, and if possible these would number zero.

(43) Source of Joy

The source of the greatest joy in life is also the source of the greatest sorrow, not that the source has changed, but that my understanding has broadened.

The rise of women's activity in what once was man's domain is in part a result of man's abdication of his leadership obligations.

This abdication by man has caused grief in many other areas.

(44) News and Media

At the present time the news media and their policies are our greatest enemy. They are destroying our faith in our nation. Their going into history and attacking our past presidents' characters. If all the heroes of the past who bolstered our patriotism, making us feel a pride in our heritage, are law breakers and liars what hope do we have for the future?

We just as well carry a gun to school. What's wrong with drugs? Why go to school? If I should learn a trade, there are no jobs to be had. The future is bleak, dull and hopeless. There is very little good about America.

(45) Only the names have been changed to protect the guilty.

A hot summer day
    Early in the morn
Clean-up the yard
    Clear down to the barn.

We toiled and we sweat
    Pulled all the weeds
The big boss watching
    Checking all our deeds

The work it lasted
    And lasted some more
My young back ached
    And my hands were sore.

The hard work done
    The hot toil finished
Our bodies weary
    Our spirits diminished

Then a bright idea
    Hit like a clap
Some on chairs
    Some on the lap

The beginning of fashion
    Even the morn
Thorup's Beauty Salon
    Is born.

There was the expert
    With the deep sweeping wave
The boys didn't care
    But the girls would rave

The marcel came next
    And the versatile bob
That seemed to fit
    Anywhere on the knob!

When the "Mod" hairdresser
    Her fury had sown
There emerged on the scene
    That famous "Wind Blown"

The heat and toil
> Pressed fashion to the top
That soothing ---cooling,
> Ever-loving "Dew-drop".

Things I remember ---Doris, written by Theo.

(46) A Guide to the Scriptures

Early in the year, a group of men met under the direction of the Church Education Department, for the purpose of revising the "Guide to the Scriptures." The group was made up of Seminary Teachers' with the exception of myself. It was an exciting experience and John was to blame for my opportunity. Thanks John.

Once in a while people review their lives and find others have had an influence for good. Some even have the character permitting them to recognize and express this good turn. Letters pasted in my journal attests to this.

(47) Our Family Unit

The level of tolerance maintained in our group is commendable. Let's not strain good will, but always be considerate.

1990 was a good year. We had great times; some problems; but no tragedies. As a family we have progressed. I know our Father in Heaven is proud of us as a unit.

(48) Dear "Good Buddy" 1/31/94 [to TJ III]

Sounds to me as if you're involved in "CB" radium

The hardest part of living here is the distance between us and loved ones. Our home is a miracle. Everything we touch, everything we see, is a reminder of a wonderful family.

That helping hand always near is certainly missed. We may never have that again, but we will always have our memories.

That show in Vegas WOW!

Each of my grandchildren, in their own way, are terrific.

I have never had a CB. I had an amateur radio license. My call letters were K7CQP. Amateurs generally tried to make a word out of their letters.

Love ya tons, see you in about a week. If you really need an excuse to come up, I'll let you play with my train.

Love, Grandpa.

(49) Christ

I have thought from time to time that I might write something that would have the depth to sway the minds of men. Milton's "Paradise Lost" is considered to be in the top ten of the world's best. I mention him only to help establish a standard. It helps a great deal if the message is delivered by a talented person.

I have also thought of the Lord, Jesus Christ. The thoughts he expressed, and the manner of delivery. I am certain His teachings will outlast all others and that the best I can do is to be an advocate for Him. The greatest service I can perform is to urge my children to do the same.

(50) My Reward

My reward depends on me,
How well I bear the load
The importance is the key
Whatever be the road

To do a job big or small
And do it really well
Start with vim and Never fall
'Till Peter rings the bell

O' what a job I could do
What effort I'd put forth
I'd turn them out two by two
And maybe even more

I'd cut a swath wide and deep
I'd run circles around them all
I'll get done while others sleep
My work would never stall

All this and more I could do
If the job were really big.
As a Bishop I'd be true
Importance is the jig (thing)

My assignment isn't much
I work at it now and then
To do my job requires NO touch
My work requires little yen.

(51) Lack of Talent

When we are found without talent, we elevate the common place through ritual and fanfare. Awards from the talent impoverished have meaning only for those with no talent.

(52) Dear John,

If you are wondering about the bailing twine on your package, yes, I put it there.

Boy are you indoctrinated! Mom and I spent 19 years doing our level best just to do that!!!! Can you imagine a loving father whose son is about to put his hand in a machine that will hurt or maim him and not warn him? To warn him or explain would be indoctrination.

How can a boy be a free thinker if his parents are going to bias his thoughts by telling him that fire burns? You say this analogy is poor? I think not. Your indoctrination is nothing but an extension of this example. I found something good and passed the news on to you. The things I found to hurt, I warned you about. It's just that simple?

You will find that wherever, for whatever anyone does something that departs from the normal, he will be criticized.

Definition of normal: Do nothing, don't become involved, don't commit yourself, don't stand for anything, criticize everyone, everything – offer no solution.

I am not bitter – I am not normal. The finest persons I have met have been people.

We, all of us, are thrilled with your efforts, your development and your attitude. We are pleased that you have had a share in the bringing of joy into the lives of a few people.

Just in reading this letter over I discover indoctrination is still running high.

Here's a load for you – I know God lives, as well as I know fire is hot!! Knowing this, should I let the whims of society change my aims in this life, rob me for eternity?

Thanks for your letter.

So long, Dad

(53) Maturity

When we desire to become an adult, overcomes our desire to remain an infant, we begin to mature.

We all live in a state of retardation. The degree of which is determined by desire. This retardation is not the result of a physical handicap, it is the degree of mental achievement compared with, or associated with, mental effort.

To clarify the statements we can graph the maturity area if we use the Olympic long jump for illustration. The long jump has the basic objective - how far can you jump – what distance can you span by running and leaping before gravity pulls you back to earth.

The factors to consider are speed, and height if we assume the earth to be the base line. We can use the take-off, and return as the contact point, and the arc between as a "defined area".

The "defined area" would be increased by running faster before take-off, or expending greater effort in gaining height, which would result in a greater distance before tough down.

The "learning defined area" could be measured with a test concerning that discipline.

The "Maturity defined area" would be determined by behavior. This brings us back to desire.

Desire leads us to purpose, the two bring us to maturity.

(54) Reflections of a Mother of 13 (11/6/77)

Maybe I can help someone else in raising their children by putting in writing a few experiences.

Sacrament Meetings and Sunday Schools were never any two alike, I spent much time in the halls or at the back of the chapel.

Daddy was active in the wards we lived in and always held a position in church that left me alone for meetings. I am not complaining and I never did. I was happy for every calling Theo had.

As each child grew older, my problems were of course lessened but still babies are babies.

I recall my first fun times, we lived in the South Grand Ward in Murray – which later was changed to Murray 6th ward. Theo was in the Sunday school and sang in the choir so I was alone with five babies. (John being 6, Elaine 4 ½, Jay 3, Joanne 1 ½, and Eileen newborn.) If the baby or Joanne fussed, I would have to get up and walk out and all the little ones followed after me. Out to the foyer we'd go and in this ward the chapel was up a flight of stairs. So I took the children and lined them up on the stairs and there they sat until meeting was over; with their arms folded. I heard most of the meetings but the important thing was that the children remembered that they were in the House of the Lord. <u>Never</u> were they allowed to run around or anything to cause disturbance.

This really wasn't a problem as each child learned this as soon as he or she was old enough to understand. As I remember many ladies brought their children out and they ran up and down the stairs and my older ones would watch them and then their little eyes would be turned to mine to see what I thought of what they were doing. I just smiled at them and shook my head as if to say, "You're being good kiddies. Just keep it up."

In South Jordan Theo (Daddy), taught Sunday school and was in the Bishopric so I never had his help there. He left in the mornings early and I dressed them and got them to church.

When John and Elaine were old enough to help it was much easier at church. I could get up with the baby and stand in the back and walk or jiggle the baby. I couldn't leave the chapel long or the smaller children would cry or become restless and forget to sit still. John and Elaine did fine as long as the little ones saw me. I think the fondest memories I have of those days were those when I was standing in the back and keeping an eye on one two, three, four, five, six and one little snow white heads filling a complete row sitting reverently, every once in a while looking back to see if I was still there for a reassuring smile and a nod saying "good girl" or "be a good boy."

One lady from a different ward knew me well but I didn't know her. She lived by the ward and she told me years later that she used to stand each Sunday in her window just to watch me drive up to church and get out of the car. "Your children are so sweet with their white hair and clean as a shiny penny."

If they only known what I had gone through to get there!

(55) INTOLERANT INTOLERANCE

I is for the Eyes I have upon you
N is for the Nose I'm looking down
T is for the Tears I'll bring upon you
O means Only that you are a clown
L is for Little ways you annoy me
E means Ever will I implore you
R is for Reluctant you'll always be
A is for Apt and that is not you
N is for Nice just as you see me
T is for the Trials you've caused me to bear
  Put them all together

(56) Sparkle and Bubble [Christmas 1970 to Elaine in Atlanta Georgia]

Sparkle and bubble from head to toe
Eager and anxious her way to go
Beware the unsuspecting soul
Whose path may block her goal.

This was my little girl, age two.
These traits blossomed as she grew
Little by little she came to know
Other folks have their way to go.

It isn't ease – a father's pride
Her own willful way to set aside
But she will learn and grow to know
And father's pride will grow and grow.

Bubble and sparkle will have their way
Directed, controlled, matured they say
And as the years come down like rain
They'll bring a flood of joy from Elaine.

      Dad

(57) Poem to Jay

I have a son, tall and strong
He's been gone – not so long

Of late his life has been awhirl
Run, turn, no, no, that's a girl

Pressures and excitements fade
Now he's left to pull the grade

Now there's time to look around
Just how in this world he's found

Oh it's great to be on my own,
My little faults don't bring a groan.

I come and go as I please
Hold it fella, at ease!

What a mob, push and shove
You'd think they'd show some love

Why do they irritate me so?
Is there no other way to go?

Yet, for me it's not so bad
Elaine's the one that really sad

Sick for home, twisted – leg
Spreading the gospel on a peg

Of that sickness I'm not prone
There goes a girl, looks like Joan

Back to work, things to do.
Did someone call "Boy Blue?"

There it is, I must confess
Homesick, lonely, yes, yes.
But don't tell anyone.

(58) Mission

I left my home and loved ones dear,
To serve the Lord – and yet I fear,
My singleness of mind was not
Exactly as we know it ought.

While tracting in a muggy May
 A tall old man in every way
Reminded me of Grandpa Dear
Oh, how I wanted him to hear
The story of the Gospel right
So this fine man might see the light!
My heart sank down to the floor
 The day he said "Don't call anymore!"

Another day that very same May,
A small white home in every way
 Reminded me of things and home,
I wonder, has the baby grown?
Do the children's toys the house 'ore spread?
Front room floor, the tub the bed?
In answer to our knock we found,
Tobacco smoke and coffee ground.

How many times do I learn?
That everything must come in turn,
That some emotions swift and strong
Are triggered by a word or song?
And really only bring to mind
Things or loved ones left behind,
Father, though' my faults I feel,
My desire to serve is real

(59) Forgiven

He said, "Forgive I pray thee"
"Not yet," I said, "Not yet".
"Your wrong is gross, you'll pay me."
"Your sin should earn your sweat."

Life is hard, as you will learn
We hold our standards high
Forgiveness will come in turn
But yours is not yet nigh

If we would dwell with our Lord
We know the climb is steep.
No weakness in us can be stored
If heaven we would reap

Thru the years we hold our grip
Our goals more ridged grow
Never will there be a slip
We're on the road we know
As ye judge, ye shall be judged
Came ringing in my ear.
As ye judge ye shall be judged
And now the meaning clear

I am a fool, an awful fool.
Why had I Lost my heart
Here I am a Satan's tool
I played the Devils part

If all my thoughts were thoughts of home
More loving would I be
If all my thoughts were thought of home
More useful would I be.

(60) How did it Happen

How did it happen, this new found thing
To penetrate, to make my heart ring
My soul leaped within me turn on turn
And then my whole being began to burn

How exciting, and then, how profound
It fills me till my ears pound and pound
It propels me, makes me want to do
I want to pass this feeling to you.

The more I give the more mine grows
Where this expansion ends no one knows
This feeling known by the discerning
I'll never forget my first burning.

(61) Parenthood

Parenthood is shunned by some.
Responsibilities do come.
Why ask for more than your share?
Living is enough to bear.
Why taste that joy so sublime,
That seems sweeter with time?
I know I'd rather be "odd"
And be a partner with <u>God.</u>

Theo and Doris

(62) How often are we Led Astray

How often are we led astray?
By worn out or false cliché'
They say a man with son so tall
Can never talk to him at all

I find that if it's really true
It all depends on me and you
The door to my soul is open wide
And you are welcome, come inside

I will admit it's an awesome sight
But if you're not prone to fright
A wealth of experience lies within
It's all yours for the rememberin'

Why should you walk your road alone?
To stumble, Tumble, bruise and groan
While I have memorized the signs
That led to a better life than mine

All these things I freely give
It's up to you just how you live.
All these thoughts are spawned of love
Pattern set by God above.

(63) Anniversary

The years have come and gone their way
    Since Cupid shot his dart,
And made your goals a common one
    By joining heart to heart.

And one by one as we have come
    To make our family circle,
We've watched the things you say and do
    And learned to see your purpose.

Perhaps at times we've made it hard
    Your noble goals to reach,
But in your might you've shown us right
    True values tried to teach.

It really has been fun for us
    To mark this special date
And with a symbol of our love,
    To show you how you rate.

The book said one's a paper gift
    (We missed that altogether);
And five years should be something wood;
    Each years a little better.

This year should be for China ware
    (You see, we're really versed);
And could you see our attitude
    You'd know that you rate first.

But now that Johnny's mission's here
    And home needs take the front,
We thought we'd forego the pleasures
    And help you take the brunt.

So if Dan Cupid's still around
    With his professional dart
He'll bear our message fond and true
    And join us heart to heart.

Happy Anniversary!

(64) Leadership

Now you walk the lonely path
of leadership,
And all the facets are not in
your grip.

The uneasiness and the
uncertainty
Leave you feeling inadequate
and empty

And yet, you know your course
is true
How you live and what you do.

To pass the word that man
might live
A chance at eternity give.

(65) Flesh of my Flesh

Flesh of my flesh, wit of my wit
Bone of my bone, mine every whit.
Search for adventure turning sour?
How do you face the quiet hour?

Bone of my bone, flesh of my flesh
When will the facets of life mesh?
How long the search for things you have?
The quiet hour will be the Salve.

In all your growing, grow closer
Maturing will be the choicer
Flesh of my flesh, bone of my bone
You're mine, in rags or on a throne
[This line replaced by the line below]
I long for the day your way will be home.

(66) Love you Illusive Thing

O Love, you illusive thing
Your pendulum is fast to swing
An arch that reaches the sublime
Turns, and races t'ward the grime

In my youth 'twas fickle fate
That brought me there, always late.
To gather in that tender joy
Providence reserved for boys

Age crept on me unawares
And Understanding climbed the stairs
To bring into my jumbling mind
A feeble light of some kind

There is a way to extend
The ruthless swing on loves end
To press my hand through the glass
That wiley pendulum to clasp

And with a tender gentle strength
In unselfishness at length
Not with Pride but Humility
Loves pendulums controlled by me.

(67) Life

I walk the street and wonder
What is life all about?
Is man for gain and plunder?
Honor him who shouts?
Where is the word Charity!
Or more, the meaning of
And where is your parity
Show what's born of love

(68) Teach my Child

I teach my child and watch him grow
With scab and bruise he comes to know

The rein is loose but not too long
Err he will, but no great wrong

The plan I use is not mine
How well I copy will tell in time.

(69) Dreams

In Dreams a horse grows taller
With power beyond belief
In dreams a dragon is smaller
And bound to come to grief

Enough of life has passed my way
I see things as they are
The gilt and glitter loaned by dreams
Out classed the thing by far

There's things I am
And things I'm not
And things I'll never be
And the things that once loomed so bright
Now mean much less to me

And now I see again
The thing that I had judged
New values come to light
I once had thought a smudge

(70) The Gods

Do the Gods looking down on the works of man
      Shake their heads and wring their hands?

Where is the means to make man see?

What is good and what is futility?

They give men the rules and let them run
      To see who builds and who's for fun

I teach my child and watch him grow
      With scab and bruise he comes to know

The reign is loose, but not too long
      Err he will but no great wrong

The plan I use is not mine
      How well I copied will tell in time.

(71) My Youth

In my youth I stood alone
To make mistakes I was prone
The shame cut me to the core
In chagrin I vowed – no more

How well do pride and shame mix?
Will a lie, chance vent the fix?
How do others do so well?
Was I born beneath a spell?

I'll shun my friends, hide from sight.
They do so well – I'm a fright.
In a new land I'm not known
Where no stumble seeds I've sown

I'll change my way over night
Dismiss the spell, end my plight
Be like others, firm and true.
Head held high, no act to rue

In a bigger world I knew
I learned to care, and I grew
I know now that others fear
The same sin that brought my tear

I came to know and like myself
For the good, not for the pelf
To love, to care for neighbor

Sweet joy is mine to savor

Not because perfections mine
I stretch to peer over grime
Correct my faults as I can
Accept myself as I am

(72) Integrity

In appreciation for your integrity in the Gospel of Jesus Christ

No man should pass through this life without leaving his contribution to the building of this world.

The gaining of wealth – position – fame or any gains for personal gratification is not a real contribution. Rationalization or justification because of side effects does not fill the requirements.

How many times must a man be born.

(73) Time is a sometimes thing

I've seen the times when it raced like mad,
And the times it would not move
And times when it splits itself and races from the half in the groove

In the year you've been gone we've had wars and treaties and many a thing
Still, on the other hand it's been dull and drab deep inside my being.

You're really not needed for the day to day chores they seem ever done

It's just somehow your glow's not here nor brought by the rays of the sun.

(74) A Walk Back in History

If I could walk back in history and see things are they were –
If I could speed into the future and know things as they'll be.
If I could, in my mind's eye, bring the two together.
I could somehow display the oneness of it all.

(75) What is a Hankie?

It entertains the babe who loves peek-a-boo
Folded and rolled it's a hammock or canoe
It's pinned to dress front with skirts flowing
It wipes the chin and aid in nose blowing

A thing attached to teens is uncool.
Sometimes is misplaced between home and school.
And when we're at church it's the whispered plea,
Daddy did you bring a hankie for me?

Love, Dad

(76) Love

Love, joy, pain, anguish, sin,
Happiness, sorrow, peace
Here and hereafter is a direct
Result of our own actions.

As we achieve a level of Love, we reap an equal level of joy. All things we reap, we earn. If we cannot understand love, we cannot feel love. Learning to love is step by step.

If your cup runneth over, maybe your cup is too small.
If my cup is too small, how do I enlarge it?
Who has the largest cup ever known?
How did they achieve their big cup?
The cup, large or small must be purchased.

(77) Priesthood Song

How can I say in words so strong?
How can I sing the priesthood song?
How can I explain power divine?
Vested in a soul meager as mine.

How can I pass power unknown?
How can I tell what's not my own?
The magnitude I cannot tell,
But in my scope I work quite well.

Allegiance, power, love supreme
All in eternity it seems
A loving Father aids the son
Anticipates the day they're one.

And so I struggle, hope and pray
The father will help find the way
To live, and love and emulate
That I may enter at the gate.

Then I, with understanding pure
Will take the help of purpose sure
Begin again the priesthood song
And bring to God, sons true, sons strong.

(78) I Will --For Ty

Consider the wise and the great
They take their food from a common plate
And similar knives and forks they use
With similar laces they tie their shoes.
The world considers them brave and smart,
But you've all they had when they made their start.

Your beginning is as theirs was, Ty,
You can give it your all, or just get by.
Courage must come from the soul with in.
God has equipped you for life, but He
Let's you decide what you will be.
No one gets anywhere standing still,
So start from the top and say, "I will."

(78) The Sleeping Sitter [Wendy holding Cali]

When grownups get together

And talk of lofty things,

I slip away with baby

When she talks, she sings.

She doesn't really know the

Words she just enjoys the sound.

I pretend to understand

And make my eyes go round.

We find the old bean bag

To cuddle up and talk.

I run my fingers in her hair–

That one little lock.

I don't know what to think

As she looks into my eyes

Her eye lids start to droop—

She makes those little sighs.

I'll just sit and hold her,

Let her sleep a while.

Her skin is soft and smooth.

Hey, she made a smile!

Wonder why her breath's so sweet?

I really like the smell.

If I have children when I'm grown,

I hope I do…as…well…

Theo John Nielsen

(79) Spiritual Experience 1971- Doris

On my way to Johns and Lorraine's home in Provo I had an experience which I shall never forget, nor will Wendy and Kathleen. Wendy was five years old at this time and Kathleen was fifteen.

John and Lorraine were both going to B.Y.U. and working besides. Christie was just a couple of months old and John and Lorraine tried to work their schedules so that John could watch Christie while Lorraine went to school, etc.

A few days a week, classes and work clashed so I drove down and stayed with Christie 'til one or the other came home.

One day, I drove the red Chevy pickup down and Kathleen and Wendy were with me. The freeway speed limits were 45 to 65 at that time but I cheated and went 40 miles an hour. I always felt safer going at least 5 under the speed limit. As I turned off the freeway I put my foot on the brakes to slow down and the pedal went clear to the floor of the car. "NO BREAKS!!"

Again and Again I pushed my foot on the brakes, but still no brakes. The off ramp was shorter than most and a bit downhill so instead of slowing down I think I may have picked up a bit of speed.

I really panicked but Kathleen realized a bit the situation and asked what she could do. All I remembered saying was, "Get Wendy and get down on the floor." Kathleen said after that I said, "Say your prayers" – which they both did.

I knew it was up to me to do the best I could. With Prayers in my heart I kept one hand on the horn in hopes of warning the cars ahead of me that I couldn't stop. As I came to the end of the ramp I made a right hand turn in hopes of avoiding a collision. I stayed as far off the road as I dared and I had finally decided to run into a fence just a head so with one last try, I put my foot on the brake and we stopped instantly.

I sat for a few minutes, to gain my composure and then drove to a service station to have the brakes checked. The service station attendant checked the brakes and could find nothing wrong. He said sometimes dirt gets on them for a bit and maybe that's what happened.

I don't know but I tried everything and I know that my prayers were answered as we came off the freeway, missing cars and then the decision to run into the fence. This much I do know, my prayers were answered. My precious children were unhurt. I was able to go on and tend Christie although I did sit and cry when I got there.

(80) My day at the Branch Genealogy Library, 4/7/1978

I was to open the library and be there to help anyone who came in.

The Stake house (where the B.G.L. is) was in the process of changing all of the locks on all of the doors. Including our microfilm closets. The janitor, opened the library door and let me in and then informed me that she had no key for the closets.

"Well, I have to have them open as we have people coming in to use the Library."

"Well," she said, "I'm sorry but I guess you can't open today. I have no key. I don't know what to do."

I said "I guess we need to pray." She laughed and said, "Well, I'll look in the closet on the other side of the hall". So we both left and went and looked. Well, there were dozens of keys but they were all old. I still wasn't giving up and she knew it. So she said, "You go back thru the chapel and close both doors and I'll look in the other closet." So we separated and I said a prayer in my heart. "Please, we must have this library open for the public to use."

Well, we met at the library and she had no luck. "I'm sorry Doris" and I said "Oh there just has to be a key here that will open these closets so I picked up the old ring of keys and tried 3 of them and the 3rd key opened the lock. The second door kind of was hard but it opened too. So I opened 3 of them but couldn't open the other. She worked and got it open. I found out later that another librarian tried every key and could not lock it before closing up that night. So on Saturday the Janitor had to lock it up with the new keys.

I know that my prayers were answered because my desires and prayers were righteous.

(81) Our Trip to Disneyland.

Our vacations were few, far between and nothing more than a trip to the mountains. For several reasons. 1 – We had been the first 10 or 15 years without paid vacations so Theo didn't take them. 2 – We didn't have money to go anywhere. 3- No car large enough for all of us to get in at once. 4 – I was either expecting or just had a new baby so – we stayed home.

My sister was living in California and was in the process of moving back to Salt Lake and her husband brought a load up in his station wagon and a rented trailer on back. In order to get a refund of $80.00, she asked if we would bring the trailer back and we could use their station wagon to transport us to Disneyland and we could stay at their place while there.

Well, I jumped at the chance and Theo talked to his employer and in less than a week we were on our way to Los Angeles (or Arcadia) a small town about 25 miles from Los Angeles.

We were so anxious to go. We really worked hard to get ready. Not even time to sew new clothes. Eileen had just started work so she and Elaine stayed home.

So in the evening after Theo got off from work, Theo, Nine children and I climbed in the car with sandwiches and snacks and left for California. As we started on the Freeway I remembered we had left without prayer so I reminded Theo and we pulled off the freeway in Draper just a few miles north of the prison and had prayer. Asking Our Heavenly Father to accompany us on our trip. Little did we realize how grateful we would be as our trip progressed that we had stopped for prayer.

Our trip went well to St. George. Theo driving to this point.

[Mom's journal entry ended here, but we feel it is important to include what happened on our drive. Someone took over the driving so that Dad could get some sleep. Sometime during the drive at night, the terrain changed and the car and trailer nearly jackknifed. In answer to our prayer earlier, no one was hurt and the car and the trailer were not damaged. Dad took over the driving and we had a fun vacation in California!]

(82) March 7, 1948 Elaine's Birth

Sunday. I had already made one trip to the hospital to have my baby and I was being prompted to go again. When I arrived at the hospital they hesitated to admit me as "it would be hours yet." But they finally did admit me but didn't notify the doctor.

As things progressed, Theo became upset with the nurse and said "If you don't call the doctor I will." So they checked me and the race was on. One nurse went to call the doctor and another proceeded to move me to the delivery room. I was already for delivery when the nurse came in and said, "The doctor was in church – what do we do now?"

Well, the nurse told me to hold my breath and tied my legs together and I was left alone in the room for 1 hour. A clock was on the wall in the room. Well, I was nearly scared to death and needed some help and looking at the clock which said 10 to 5 I remembered praying for help to endure – Honestly and Sincerely.

As I prayed a thought or (vision) came to me so real and I saw Mother standing there and I immediately realized how hard my mother labored to have each one of us and she could do it. It was what I needed and I became calm.

At the same time, a Japanese nurse appeared in the door way and saw what the other nurses had done to me. She hurried over called for help and released my legs and my baby was delivered. The intern came in and put me out almost as quick. When I came to the doctor was there and I was ready to go to my room. Everything fine.

As they wheeled me into the hall I saw Theo standing there with Mama. I said. "When did you get here?" She said, "About 10 to 5:00. I felt you needed me."

(83) May 2, 1962 – Ty's Birth

6 Weeks before Ty was born, the doctor informed me Ty was turned wrong and warned me of a hard delivery.

Mom and Dad as usual were worried and concerned so Dad asked if I'd like a Father's Blessing. Which I, of course, asked for a blessing and received a very special Father's Blessing. One promise was to rest and not worry because the baby would turn and be delivered normally!

Six weeks later I entered the hospital with the baby still wrong. The doctor was there but informed me he could not help or he might hurt the baby as well as me. He was going down to get lunch then he'd be back. I always had terrific headaches after my babies were delivered but this time I got it before delivery and I asked the nurse if I could have an aspirin. She came in and hurried out and caught the doctor at the elevator. He came back and checked my blood pressure and asked if I had ever had a headache like that before (My blood pressure was sky high and he was concerned.) I told him I had them after but never before. Well, he said, "I guess we better help you. I can't let your blood pressure be up like this so he said to the nurse I'll check her you go get the delivery room ready, etc.

As he was examining me he said. "Doris, are you going to have twins?" or "Doris, this is a miracle. Your baby has turned and will be delivered normal. He went to the door and called Theo in and said, "Theo come in and witness a miracle. The baby has turned and will be delivered normal."

Theo with a grin said, "Well, That's what we expected wasn't it?" And the Doctor said, "No, there is no room in the birth canal for a baby to turn. It is a miracle."

Theo called Dad and informed him. The Baby is fine and was delivered Normal!

■ ■

Beth in the Ocean

Marty's being healed from Asthma (Daddy's prayers answered)

Eileen's Mission (I prayed to take her pain)

Kathleen deciding to go on a mission (Bishop Jackman)

(84) Part of Grandma's 1992 Year end summary

53 Grandchildren and 2 Greatgrandchildren for us. How blessed we are. All such special and beautiful babies. They are all so different in size and looks, but each one is so beautiful and their little spirits radiate beauty and love. How could anyone not want one of God's spirits?

Our selling our home has made mixed emotions. We had many really special times there. A nice place for our children and I thing even better for the grandchildren. We were away from the busy streets. It all happened so fast. I really didn't think we'd sell it. But everything just kept moving. First part of October we settled on the home and had three days to get out. Thanks to the family, we had one more Family Home Evening which was so special. Tears and love abound. Then came the building of our house. Such a long ride for everyone and work, work, work!. Everyone has wanted to come in and see this "instant" house.

We witnessed miracles or blessings every day they worked on it. Sometimes it was really cold for everyone but no complaints were heard. Just work faster!

Some of the people up here that helped or just stopped in told us that they have never seen a group work together like that. We told them that they were our family and they said that too was a miracle.

Well, whatever it was, I was and am so proud of all those tires backs that came home so late to eat and get some rest.

My house, I hope will soon be a home. So much love put into it, I love it and as I go from room to room I am reminded of our blessings. Thanks to all of you. I don't believe a day goes by that one or the other of us comments how nice it is. If we could just be a bit closer.

We love you all so much. You're welcome anytime! Still plenty of room, but no trees yet. Hopefully, we'll get something this spring.

…The conditions in the world are terrible. I find myself saying, "Why can't people change and then there I am."

So I guess the answer is study, pray, work if you can, and try to keep our Father in Heaven's commandments. Which if kept, just bring peace, love and happiness.

I pray that if I can help anyone in need (of anything) I will be engaged in right and helping. I sure love all of you. I am grateful for you. I truly know I have been blessed.

(85) Dear Family,

I want to tell you some reasons why I am what I am. Some of the reasons I do not know myself unless it be weakness on my part.

First – I want you to know, I believe I am a child of God. I believe Christ hung on the cross for us. That Moses crossed the sea on dry ground – That Noah built an ark. I have <u>never</u> had one doubt of these things.

> My Dad – (affectionately so called) to me was a great <u>man</u>. Yes, he did have <u>one</u> fault I saw and it was his temper. I believe it was as sad a thing to him as it was to me. But never was there a more appreciative man, loving, <u>honest,</u> understanding, harder working, and tender than Dad. He had harsh ways some times that I didn't understand as a kid (I understand now but I do not say it was right.) His little tender ways were so special. Like the prettiest rose in the garden he would pick and bring into Mom and say some little sentimental thing to her as he gave it to her. I guess this is one reason the rose is so special to me today.
>
> Dad was a well-read man. He worked from day-lite 'til dark – Then the paper was read and he found time to study the scriptures. Another thing he enjoyed was Natl. Geographic's. I think Dad had a good knowledge of the Gospel. Many people came to Dad for answers to gospel questions. But Dad lived his religion everything was either right or wrong! Yes or no. There was <u>no</u> half way in anything for my Dad. Bad? No. We definitely knew what his stand was. Never did we try to talk Dad into changing his mind once he said no.
>
> Mother – Just as hard a worker, talented in every way. She made all our clothes, she played the piano, she crocheted, quilted, canned 1,000s of quarts of fruit and vegetables each year, painted and papered for herself and many people in the ward just to help them out. We picked berries and I remember the cups were stacked high as Mom and Dad sold them for extra help. Mother never complained about her health but as I remember her she <u>never felt good</u>. She was a person that couldn't just sit. She always had projects near every chair. And her hand work was <u>beauty</u>! Mother's main quality I think was keeping your word at any cost. I don't believe Mother ever refused help of any kind to anyone.
>
> As you can see Mom and Dad were alike in many ways but the one way that we were always sure of was they stood by each other. Mother could correct us by "Do you want me to tell your Dad" and we soon straightened up. Yes! I was somewhat afraid of Dad but only because he expected us to do what we should. And we knew to be told twice was a sin.

We did many things that were hateful as kids that most kids and I admit my sisters and brothers say it too. I probably did then too. But as I look back now. Oh what choice times – Our Family Orchestra

        Family Month to Clean the Ward House
Working in American Fork
        Picking Raspberries early in AM
Sep. Chaff from the beans in winter.
        Picking currants - An all day job.
Hoeing in the hard soil that Dad dug by hand.
        Cleaning the corral
Wall papering for neighbors
        Helping people house clean. Etc.

Well, as a child I didn't have a special friend like my girls and boys did. We were made fun of. We were called "Billy Goats" etc. But we didn't care (most of us) because we had brothers and sisters. All the neighbors came over because we had fun playing. We made up games and made our work fun.

At school I ate lunch with my sisters and their friends. I remember we didn't have a lot of clothes but even then I knew they were made with love. Mother made me slips out of flannel because I was sick so much but I remember her crocheting an edge on the hem. I wasn't one to fix hair and the like.

I guess you might think we never played because I think I worked hard, to what the children of today do. But we did! Mother couldn't work in the hot sun so we worked until it got hot and then we used to sit out on the front porch or out on the south lawn which was edged with Lilacs. Here I learned to appliqué quilt blocks and embroider. Wilma taught 4-H one year and I went and learned to darn stockings. I made my first pair of bloomers.

Well, this is getting long but what I wanted to do was tell you why I react to some things like I do.

When work was to be done we did it. On a farm you don't usually have a choice when.

Work was work. Play was play, not your job, not man's job just do it and <u>do it right</u>. (To the best of your ability) Yes, I did many jobs over because they weren't done like Dad thought they should be or Mom wanted them. But how proud I was when I had finished it and they said "Good".

I love work, I love life. I love to run, walk. I love babies. I always had a way with them.

"Clean the corners – the middle will take care of itself"

The trimming of the lawn is to me more important than the middle.

<u>Dusting and Sweepings just as important as washing your face.</u>

"If a thing is worth doing, it's worth doing right."

I still believe this but for some reason I can't do it now.

Maybe I didn't do what I should have years ago. I thought I was doing all I could do. Now I wish I could go back and do all those things I should have done. Yes, I think I have learned to accept pain. But I cannot handle this doing nothing. I want to run. I would do so much more than I did. I would take Terri's problem and let her go on for me.

I do love my children – each one of you. You are all different but I couldn't say one was more precious than another.

Please forgive me for the things I did not teach you that I should have. Forgive me for any neglect you may have suffered. Forgive me for any ridicule you may have had to bear for my sake.

You (had – have) a wonderful Father. He loved you too. I know we didn't always agree … He wasn't raised like I was. I always liked his Father and Mother when I was a young girl. And I think Theo's Dad liked me after Theo and I were married.

Be good kids. Love life – Love yourselves. God blessed you all with perfect bodies. Keep them that way. I am so grateful to have been given the privilege of being your Mother. I am so proud of each of you. Be proud of yourself. Don't let anyone make you feel below yourself. You are a child of God. Remember this. Don't let anyone knock that, not even a spouse! This breaks my heart. Even if you make a mistake it shouldn't make you any worse than "God's Child" –

Just one thing more – "Whatever you want to be – be the best you can." Even if it is "just" a "mom or housewife". That is important whether society downs it. Your spouse can't be their best if you aren't your best.

Remember I do love you all. I always will and I am so proud of each one of my special grandchildren. I wish I could be a better Grandma. I love you! Love Jesus, and Grandma will always be proud of you.

Lovingly Mom and Grandma

(86) 17 Dec 1982 [Doris' Journal Entry]

I am so grateful for my blessings. For my parents, my membership in the church, I am grateful for children that have clean thoughts and desires.

6:00 am Tuesday 23 August 1983

I admit I am about to the end of the rope. As far as my tolerance is. So I thought I'd tell you, my children a bit about my thoughts.

First – I know I had the kindest lovingest and thoughtful parents in this would. I wish you could have known them. Daddy was a hard worker. He loved work and always taught us that wasting time was worse than anything. Of course it must be used for good, up lifting things. He was thoughtful of others – Although his family's welfare was first he always willingly shared his time, talents and goods. To Dad, there was only right or wrong. – NO in between. <u>Dad and Mom were the best!!</u>

Mother – A sweet loving, talented, caring understanding – person. I can't describe her good enough although mother was in bad health she always helped someone she felt needed her. With dinners, sewing, wall papering, baby sitting, crocheting, or just a good listening ear.

[If you continue reading in this part of her history, she includes each of her siblings and their spouses.]

One thing about each of my brothers and sisters that I can't say enough about is commitment; they all were dedicated and stood by their beliefs. We had some ridicule as children, but most of the time we ignored it and did what we believed to be right.

I am very grateful for my brothers and sisters. My wonderful parents. I know my actions are not always good as they should. I have always said, and I do now, I was blessed by being allowed to have such wonderful parents and brothers and sisters.

Now I have a choice family. My children have benefited by my brothers and sisters. They have been blessed with an understanding and loving father. Theo is a good example for his children. I love him

No one loved their children more than I loved mine. I know I was blessed to have them. But I did keep you home. As close as my eyes could keep you. Not long away from eyesight.

I felt I had to teach you and how could I without having you home?

I needed my children to help me grow. I always knew we were growing together as my children taught me so much. Not always in words – deeds, but experiences in life.

I love each one of you and am proud of you and the way you are teaching your children. I am not saying I agree with all of your ideas but I pray if I am wrong, you are right.

I love the Church of Jesus Christ of Latter Day Saints. I don't know how anyone can survive without it. We definitely must have a purpose – a goal – And keep working on it.

I hope if I should go before Daddy you would all be good to him. Help him – He finds it hard to ask for help. He has always done about what had to be done. If he didn't know how, he found out but seldom did he ask someone to do something for him. He appreciates all of you.

I am glad you all love your father. I have always envied his ability to tell you all off so bluntly and you didn't get mad. Just loved him more. He loves to be loved. He's proud of each one of you and I hear him always brag about you and your families and your goals and accomplishments.

The situation in the world is terrible. Yet we are told if we live the Gospel we do not have to be of the world. It is odd how different each child takes or accepts this. Some will handle it fine! Others can't seem to handle it at all. They are still grasping that precious Iron Rod and their goals are still for a "forever" family but it is hard and they are trying. I feel they all know but some are taking a lot of knocks along the way.

The choices our youth and even adults have to make these days are unreal. Science has so much knowledge but where is it leading us? Are we all lacking "True Faith"? I pray this is not so. Medicine in ways seems to be back sliding, yet they can do so much more for people than when I was a child - or even when having my family.

8 April

What a special treat this conference is. It is too bad we can't have this every day. Spirit Food is sure what we all need and definitely what we need.

(87) History [Theo]

I was born in a small town – Spring Lake, Utah. On the 20th day of January 1922. Our house was on a 40 acre farm. Dad went for the doctor on a horse named "Jack." I was a very cross baby. She fed me honey on a feather.

When still young we moved to Salt Lake because Dad lost the farm. He was able to get a job at a meat packing plant. Cudehy. The family tired of the big city when I was 5 years of age. We build a home in Santiquin, Utah. Dad had gotten a better job at Linde Air Products. He stayed with a sister during the week, but spent the week ends in Santiquin.

While in Santiquin, I learned to herd sheep, climb (hike) mountains, eat thistles, ride horses. We left Santiquin when I was seven and went back to the big city - Salt Lake. We then moved to Holiday then the Millcreek. We were in Mill Creek until 1937. We then moved to Wyoming. I was now 15 years old. High school in Casper was in uniform, girls and boys. Too keep from taking ROTC, I took auto mechanics. People thought we were funny because we were Mormons.

At seventeen I helped take the church census for the Wyoming district of the Western States mission. I traveled with the district leader (President). The work was the most interesting on the Indian reservations. We drove a model "A" Ford.

At age 18 I went to work in Pueblo, Colorado, at Linde Air Products. Dad got the job for me. Jobs were hard to find and I became rich overnight. A Mexican lady let me charge my meals until payday. She also made my lunches.

I grew tired of living at the YMCA and eating in a restaurant so I quit my job and went back to Wyoming. I worked as a welder through the summer, almost. The boss blew up a road tanker breaking his legs. Being out of work, I went to Salt Lake City and worked at Consolidated Wagon and Machine. The year was 1941. Pearl Harbor was bombed on December 7th. I quit my job and went to Indiana to see my folks before joining the navy.

Mother decided to leave Dad about that time and asked me to return to Mill Creek, purchase land and build a house. I was now 20 years old. Bird was living in Mill Creek and helped to hack a path to the new land we had purchased. $15.00 down and $15.00 per month. Total Price $1,500.00. In August I finally joined the Navy.

I was sent for "boot" training to Great Lakes near Chicago. While there Dad paid me a visit. From there I was sent to Indianapolis, Indiana to radio school. During that winter our Theory Instructor twisted his ankle skiing. Because of my training, I was asked to fill in for him until he was able to get back to work. This was a good experience and lasted some weeks.

Upon graduation, I applied for sub marine duty and I was assigned to the naval air base at Quansit point, Rhode Island. Our job there was to service the fleet air craft. We modified many planes communications wise and kept the training planes flyable.

While there I was sent to outlying fields to install communication equipment among these were Martha's Vineyard, Massachusetts, Hyades Port and Westerly Place.

This assignment lasted 10 months. I was anxious for action and was able to get assigned to the aircraft carrier Oriskiney. But before we were able to put to sea, the carrier wasp was sunk by the Japs. We were quickly re-commissioned Wasp and sent to replace the sunken

Wasp. For shake down we sailed to Trinidad from Boston. Our home port. We returned to Boston, cut our crew by about 10% and left Boston for the Pacific Theatre. Our passage through Panama Canal was interesting. We knocked over all the lamp posts along the side of the locks as we progressed. The little antique engine that pulled us along would spin its wheels and make an awful fuss. It looked more like a toy that anything else.

The culture of Panama is quite different from ours. Their standards are quite low. I'm sure there must be good people there but we did not meet them. Our stay was brief. Next stop was San Diego, California.

While in San Diego, I visited the family of a sailor whom I quite liked at Quonset Point. There were devout Catholics.

Next stop was Pearl Harbor. The signs of battle were still there. We were two days there and then left for the battle area. We struck Midway for practice on our way to Majuro.

We joined the fleet (remainder) at Majuro. We began the seemingly endless pattern of "Strike" for two days then "Run" two days. Then back to "strike." For months on end this cycle continued. There came a time when it was felt battle fatigue was wearing on the crew. We went back to Majuro, (the war far north of this area now) where we rested for several weeks. Then back to the action.

The purpose of this is not a WWII history so I'll say only this, It ended and I was discharged. Dec. 26, 1945. But before the end we were "Hit" and had to return to the states for repairs.

While waiting for the shop to be repaired I came to Salt Lake and was captured by a little blonde girl whom I married about six months later. (November 28, 1945)

Our movements, our children's arrivals are all documented for anyone interested. I will spend my efforts with events and philosophy.

(88) Christ like life

People say I should live a "Christ Like" life. This leave me to define that life. Life is made up of many facts. It isn't just bad or good. It has to be bad or good because…..

Because he was good to his mother and father. Because he loved dogs or didn't kick cats.

So what are the characteristics that made the Christ what He is?

He healed the sick. He raised the dead. He fed the hungry. I don't believe these acts tell the story.

I believe the motivation is where the answer is to be found. Jesus said that what he did was that which He had seen the Father do.

If that is the case, then we must look to the Father to see why he did the things He did. Could love the answer? Love of what?

To detail the last query, would demand another book. Let's bring it down to the present day, make the phenomenon easier to understand.

Some years ago I gave my wife a hundred dollars and asked her to buy herself some clothing. She took the money and bought clothes for the children, nothing for herself. She said hers were satisfactory.

Why did my wife spend the money on someone else?

I lived with her for 50 years and her attitude was always the same, others first. Friends, neighbors, family, acquaintance, their need was greater than her desire. She would do fine with what she had.

Once when my reluctance must have been too apparent she asked, "Don't you see? Can't you understand?"

I confess, I did neither. Today I do. The benefits of "Others First" attitude, when it becomes a real desire, is joy.

My idea of a "Christ Like" life stems from loving others at least equal to the love you have for self.

Christ did for those people in His day, and for all mankind, He did because He wanted to do them. He had a real desire. The wondrous things God the Father has done for us He has done because of unselfish love.

Have you ever wondered how Sodom and Gomora became universally wicked?

As I observe the world today, I see our morality is in a swift transition. Our acceptance of premarital sex is becoming quite wide spread and with the help of the media, is on an upward spiral.

If you have an uneven step in your stairway, you will notice the irregularity at first, but will soon take the stair without a hitch or thought.

You may stumble on a friend's stair that is without irregularity. We become accustomed to the signs and enticements of sin.

"Sin, what sin, I haven't killed anyone."

"We are consenting adults, there is no crime in that."

The language used in some homes is shocking in other homes.

By law there is no God. In our attempt to be all things to all people we have had to rule out God. The Anti God doctrine is quite legal.

Without God in our lives there is no long range hope for the human race. The environmentalists will have no worries when the Homo sapiens are extinct.

I must be a precious soul, or why would Heavenly Father have given me such a wonderful girl to help salvage me from the world?

He said every soul is precious to Him. Our lives are a testimony of His statement. When in doubt, ask Him.

(89) A Computer Techs Song

With a bent-up floppy in each drive and a c.p.u just dumped,
I tell you boys life's not so very sweet, when your jaz drive hits a bump.

The vga just laid an egg and the modems hung by a wire.

The phone is ringing off the wall with the customers desires.

(Melody by request)

(90) Traditions

Once upon a time, there was a family who was reared in tradition. The kind of traditions that involved the whole family. It was tremendous fun. And all through life everyone put their share of effort into making the occasion a real occasion.

Time crept alone and the fun of the family traditions seemed to fade away. Become less important. The older children were pulling away, doing their own thing. The family gatherings were less important.

As the next generation came to leadership in family organization, the importance of traditions dwindled and were soon forgotten.

At one time I decided not to write because whatever I might say had already been said by those who were more eloquent, and renowned. The thought strikes me that those I care most for may never read the works of those eloquent and renowned. Maybe the people I care most for will not appreciate Shakespeare or some other dead language.

The scriptures are written in an understandable language. Keep to the pure language, let slang die a deserving death.

It isn't fame or fortune that determines the measure of a man. The measure of a man is in the contribution he makes to the lives of other men.

Every time I discover a truth such as just stated I begin to write in my notes and as I do so the thought comes to mind of a scripture making the same statement. The format maybe changed, but the truth is the same.

It would be difficult to make a contribution to another life if you had no regard for that person. In other words, you must love him. At least enough to part with "yours" and make it "his."

Her explanation was, "What greater service is there than bringing a new life into the world? And if I should die in the doing, what better way is there to go?"

83

It was said by some friends that her husband ought to know better. One lady told him he should be jailed. Some of his coworkers offered to "fix" him forcibly. With this as a background ho do your judge your mother?

Expediency of the moment, Sometimes effects actions. How often are were motivated by emotion rather than reason.

Wealth is in the heart, or in the head, or in the eyes of a beautiful girl.

If I had no hope for life with Doris in Eternity, it would surely be hell.

Decisions are made by people with differing motivations. Some decisions are made and then the evidence is selected to prove the erroneous theory. Differ net motivations that promote decisions are: Reason, emotion, rational, analytical.

(91) History

In 1945 I asked Doris to marry me, I had just left her at the train depot, I even kissed her goodbye. She kissed me back. It's been 28 years and I can still feel her lips when I think about it.

The train took me from Salt Lake to Seattle, 2 days, two long days. I knew I was going to ask her the minute I found a phone. As the train pulled out, I looked at her through the window – that's when I knew. All the time we'd been together and it strikes me as the train pulled out.

I found a phone in Seattle and called her at work. She answered and so did a dozen other girls. I could hear all the receivers as the girls were told of Doris' long distance call. Of course I "chickened out" and asked her if I could call her at home that evening. She said she'd be home about 6:00.

The day worried itself out and I was back on the phone at 5 minutes to 6:00. Doris wasn't home but her mother looked up the street – she was near enough home to hear her mother call. I held on until she said "hi".

May 29, 1945 - Today I received a long distance phone call from Theo. He has asked me to be his wife. Call from Seattle. Two calls in one day.

I didn't take any chances on missing my purpose, "Will you marry me?" No answer, then "This is all so sudden" I couldn't believe it. She said she would think about it and write a letter with her answer.

The next day I was transferred to San Francisco. It was a temporary transfer to be with the air group. Uncle Sam didn't think our mail was important so he just set it aside until the ships repairs were completed and she sailed down to Alimeda (San Francisco) to pick us all up.

Well, two weeks had passed with no word from Doris. We were to sail the next day – I had to know.

I waited until Doris should be home and called again. Her answer "Of course I'll marry you!" Why couldn't she have said that two weeks ago?

June 3, 1945 - Today I received my first flowers. Pint and Orchid sweet peas and white asters from Theo. They were beautiful.

June 9, 1942 - Today I received a long distant call from Oakland, California and I told him I would become Mrs. Nielsen.

June 12, 1945 - Received a telegram saying he was being shipped.

We sailed and the war went on. We wrote every day; she wrote the news of home, while I made wild promises.

It was sometimes near a month between mailings or receiving mail. I used to open all the letters, arrange them by date, then read. As I would read a page I placed it on the bottom of the stack. When I came to the first page I proceeded to read through again and again.

The war was finally over and the problem of how to discharge men equitably. I didn't care how the politicians figured the system – I had points enough for discharge on every plan they came up with.

Our ship was off the coast of Japan, our home port was Boston. Our speed 12 knots. We stopped two days at Pearl Harbor; sailboats, sign, bands, rowboats, barges, homecoming, parties, open house, people. Transfer name your spot. I requested San Pedro, with 24 days delayed orders.

The train from Boston to Salt Lake drug the trip out to three days and managed to be five hours late.

I made a bet with a shipmate that Doris would meet the train; no matter how late it was. We finally arrived and who do you think was there to meet me? He paid off – I introduced them – he left my life. Doris was always suspicious of the meaning of that pay off.

While walking back to town Doris asked how long I would be home and when we would be married.

I had made a lot of big talk when I was far away from home and Doris, not – what do I say now? My answer was slow in coming so Doris asked if I had changed my mind. It was the day I discovered I was a "chicken-livered lover".

We made our plans, wrapped the cake and sent invitations. We were happy. I thought wrapping cake was weird especially when I found out it was to be slept on. So what? It couldn't hurt anything.

Married Wednesday, November 28, at 2:10pm in Salt Lake Temple. A beautiful day and a wonderful wedding. Nice reception in Ivan's Ward in evening.

The day before the wedding I managed to kiss Doris five times. So I said "Guess what? I've kissed you five times in one day!" She said that would be all…she meant it! I went home a little scorched. I was supposed to pick her up before 7:00 in the morning ….maybe I wouldn't show up.

How could she look so great at 6:45 am! We were on our way. The next several hours were very uncomfortable. At 10 minutes after 2 p.m. we were one. The official said I could kiss her, she didn't object.

We had our picture taken and were next busy with the reception.

Our relatives came and went and we cleaned up the chapel Doris had rented. She sent me home with a load of people and gifts in Byrd's car. I tried to warn her of the danger of leaving her to the mercy of my relatives, but she said "Go."

I didn't know where I'd find her. In a canyon? Tied to a tree? Payson jail? My family has no peers when it comes to "Chivalries.

Innocence is its own protection, she was just where I had left her. My 24 days were gone and I had to report at San Pedro.

It was Doris' first train ride. She stayed in L.A. with Alice while I was transferred to Shoemaker for discharge and payday.

This big shot gave his last 50 cents to the porter when we left the train.

We had to ride the bus home because I was no longer in the service. They would have let me on the train, but not Doris, so we came home by bus.

We had a rest stop along the way where there was snow on the ground. I hadn't seen snow for a couple of years, so my new wife washed my face in it.

There was an older woman sitting behind us on the bus who smoked and became annoyed when Doris opened the window. "Dear, would you close the window?" "I will if you will quit smoking!" The older woman agreed and our trip became more pleasant. Who said those small, soft things didn't have backbone? I had no idea at that time how much fortitude my new partner had. I'm not sure I do now.

Doris went back to work and I began to build a small house on some property I owned.

We moved in the spring. It wasn't much but it was ours. Kitchen and bedroom; cinderblock walls, coal stove and growing up.

I hadn't gone to church for years, and now I discovered I didn't really have a desire. When John was two years old I was first counselor in the Elders Quorum. My attendance at priesthood meeting was 100 percent. But only about 5 percent at Sunday school. One Sunday morning I came home from priesthood meeting changed to my work clothes, while Doris readied herself and Johnny, after the third time getting John ready, the exasperated mother said, "What's the matter with you? Every time I get you dressed, you get undressed."

About this time I received a shock that changed my life. My young son logically answered, "If Daddy don't have to go, I don't have to go." We had ten minutes, we all made it.

I had decided to skip the part of our life where we decided to get Johnny but I believe Doris' children have a right to know her.

About a week after we were married, I got brave and asked Doris how much she knew about the "Birds and Bees". She let me know she knew all she needed to know. The subject was dropped until one day she came and said she wanted a baby. Only one thing, she wanted to be sure the baby would not arrive before we had been married 9 months. I felt I could "guarantee" that.

When we found the baby was on the way Doris began calling it Johnny. I thought we might have a cute little blonde girl named Johnny, but Doris knew better, and persisted. I said I wouldn't have a kid named after me, we didn't argue, she just kept calling him Johnny.

The day he was born they showed him to me. I was very disappointed. When Doris came out of the anesthesia, she said, "Honey, Johnny's here."

"Yes."

"Who does he look like?"

"Me." (He didn't look like anyone)

"Is he cute?"

What do you tell a new mother? "Yes." What a liar I had become. The nurse laughed at me.

Then she said, "What shall we name him?" For more than 9 months we had been calling him Johnny.

We lived in our little house until after Elaine came to join us. Our neighbor lady said we were lucky to get our family in the first two tries.

I got the bug to have my own business and formed a partnership with a man. We opened for business in Cedar City, Utah. The partnership lasted about 3 months.

We moved back to Murray, into a little house behind Thorups; we had sold our home.

We then bought ½ acre from Dad Thorup and built another house. It was about 6400 south on Jefferson St.

By now we had Jay. His eyes must have had a defect – they could only see the color blue. Mom called him "Tiny Boy Blue". Grandpa called him silver because his hair was silver; it shown in the dark.

We stayed on Jefferson 5 years and added Joanne. She was just a "Button".

I went into business again– belly up again.

Eileen came. When we told people we had a dark baby they would laugh at us. Beth came next – finally! She was from April 26th to June 18th late.

About that time I came home to find no supper but fence to fence kids in my back yard – 26 of them.

"Where's supper?"

"I haven't had time, ---tending kids." She went on "all day every day."
I went out to the edge of the world and bought 20 acres with the nearest house ½ mile away.

I didn't do it because of no supper, but because my wife needed a rest from being the community babysitter.

We sold the house on Jefferson and moved to a 20x20 garage.

I didn't want to ruin my shoes pouring the concrete so I waded in the pour barefooted. If you ever have the same idea forget it. I can't remember how long it took to grow new skin on my feet.

We moved in; no water, no power, but all alone.

If anyone asks you what happiness is, it's eight people in two rooms with no conveniences. No that's not true – it's eight people who love each other. What they have or don't have doesn't matter.

The Indian migrant farm workers camped on the corner and danced and sang by their campfire. My family would sit on the hayrack watching and listening until I came home. Doris was afraid of the gas lantern and would not light it or let anyone but me. Each room was 10' x 20' with all we owned inside, except the cow that is and Dusty our Collie Dog.

The power company built us a pole line for $860.00 and we had power.

One day in mid-winter I came home from work and found my wife hanging wet clothes on the line to dry. The wind was blowing as always, the temperature with chill factor must have set the effective temperature at 10-20 below zero. It was so cold my cheeks puckered. The next day we had an electric dryer. I got a big kiss.

The water didn't come for another year. Mom chipped ice from the water barrel, melted it on the stove so we could use it.

The next spring – John and Elaine were at school. Jay and Dusty were exploring our property. Doris was feeling blue; poor little Jay out there at the bottom of the field sobbing his heart out.

Mom could see the top of his head as they made the round of the 20 acres. As they came nearer home Mom discovered Jay was not sobbing, but singing at the top of his voice. "I'm glad we live here Mom." Mom felt better about the whole thing too.

Because of the distance to work, I decided a motor bike would be a good investment. My gas bill dropped from $5.00 to .35 cents. That was great until one day a man made a left turn in front of me. The next thing I remember is looking into a ring of faces in the sky.

I tried to stand but something was wrong. Someone said "Stay Down." Next a man said, "I'm Dr. Steel from Nephi, I'm giving you a shot."

My scooter was wrecked and I had a broken leg.

Phlebitis, a month on my back, shots, hospital, home on a limp. The man I worked for had given mom $50.00 a week while I was off work, which we paid back later. It sure helped.

I felt I could milk my own cow again so I asked the neighbor, who had taken my cow a few days after the accident because he said just anyone milking her would spoil her. When could I pick her up?

When I asked him when would be the best time to pick up the cow, he said to wait awhile maybe a couple of weeks. I did and then approached him again and he said, "Why not wait a couple more weeks?" I said I was able and said I'd pick up the cow. The next day I went to his farm and he said, "Before we go to the corral, I have a story to tell you."

"The day after I took your cow, she was jostled off the bridge and got a sliver in her leg which I didn't notice until a few days later when she was infected. She went from bad to worse until she was down. The Vet said let her die. She's as good as dead anyhow. Even though she was down, I kept milking and feeding her. Now what I want you to do is pick any cow in my herd as a replacement."

I said I'd just take mine and do the best I could with her. She eventually got well and came back in her milk.

(92) All about Dogs – Buster

"When I was very young my father found a better job. It was a good job, but Dad had to work some nights. Mother was afraid when she was left alone at night, so Dad brought home a puppy dog to protect her. I liked the dog, and asked Dad what kind of a dog it was. He told me it was half lion and half tiger. That was even more exciting. I told everyone about the dogs amazing family tree.

The dog was named "Buster", and he grew to about forty pounds. When Dad played his mouth organ Buster would howl. Buster could not sing very well.

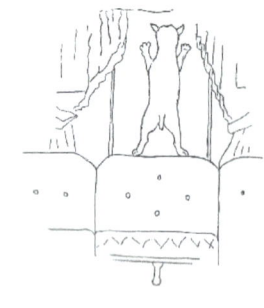

One night, when Dad was at work, Buster jumped up on the back of the couch with his feet on the window glass. He was very angry. I didn't see anything on the porch, but Buster must have thought he did.

One evening when Dad was teasing Mother, hugging her and stealing kisses, Mother told him to stop. He didn't, so she screamed. It was not a very loud scream, but she said that if he did it again she would scream louder. Buster had sprung to Mother's aid by clamping his jaws firmly around Dad's ankle. Buster was growling softly. The pause lasted several seconds. Dad released his hold, and stepped back with his free leg. Buster walked across the room to his favorite spot.

The problem with Buster was that he thought he owned the car, once he had taken possession. He sat on the seat and allowed no trespassing. Not even Mother could persuade Buster to get out of the car. If Dad was away from home Buster would sit in the car and show his authority. No amount of persuasion, coaxing, not even food would sway him. When Dad came home he would walk to the side of the car and order Buster out. He would jump to the ground and trot away.

When my father was able to buy a car, it was a used Model T Ford. The only glass on the car was the windshield. The easiest way to get into the car was to climb over the side and sit on the seat. Buster could make it in a single leap.

My father built a small picket fence in our front yard, at the edge of the grass. He said we were not to cross the fence. We could easily have stepped over the fence, but we were obedient. Buster followed our example until one day a man came down the street carrying several wooden orange crates. I don't know what upset the man, but he stooped over to pick up a rock. He threw it at Buster. The dog had been attacked. He was quickly over the fence after the man who dropped his crates and ran.

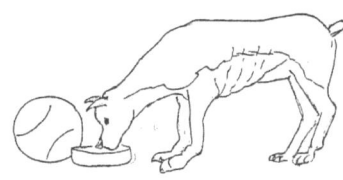

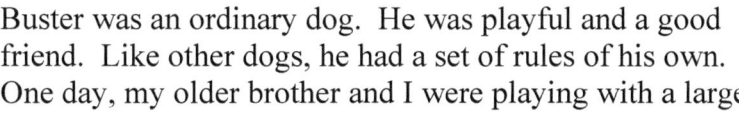

Buster was an ordinary dog. He was playful and a good friend. Like other dogs, he had a set of rules of his own. One day, my older brother and I were playing with a large brown ball. I missed the toss, and the balled rolled over by Buster who was eating his evening meal. I stooped to pick up the ball which was too close to his food, he bit my hand, puncturing my skin. I had stepped over Buster's boundary.

Buster was as fearless as any animal ever was, except for one thing, firecrackers. The morning of the Fourth of July every year he would disappear. He would be gone for almost a week, then come home hungry and tired.

Buster had another rule, he was part of the family. When the family went on a trip, he thought he had a right to go also. He would jump around dancing and barking. The one time we left him home our plans for him all went wrong.

Whether we were putting along at a twenty mile clip with Buster on the running board or jumping off the car after a squirrel and rolling over and over, Buster was as happy as happiness could be expressed.

One Fourth of July Buster did his usual disappearing act, but this time he never returned. We finally gave up on finding our friend, and never did learn his fate.

(93) Dusty from Dad's Perspective

"I think that a kid should have a dog to grow up with." Well, I said it. Now we would have to see how that little bit of philosophy impressed my wife.
After proper amount of hesitation, she said, "We need many things before we need a dog."

From a practical point of view she was right but from the viewpoint of a young father with three small children.......

"Why don't you be honest; you want the dog for yourself."
One of the traits I've always enjoyed about my lovely wife, and one of the reasons I wanted to marry her was because of her openness. You never had to wonder what she was thinking. Now that I had been exposed to the whole world, I was silent for a few moments as we rode the highway.

"What kind of dog would you get?" She was looking out the window as she said those softening words.

"A collie." I had memorized the address listed in the paper. After another quiet moment I boldly suggested we go past the place and have a look at the pups advertised. I received a crooked half grin, and an "okay".

"You coming in?"

"No. It's your dog."

I sheepishly left the car and knocked on the door. The man of the house showed the pups in the Garage. There were eight of them. As they milled around I noticed that one of the 2 largest pups was standing straight-legged, head held high; looking eyeball to eyeball at me. "Is that one a male?"

"Yes, I'll get him for you."

I bent over the barrier and the pup walked toward me. I had the dog in my possession. The temptation was too great, the man held his money and I had a dog "for my three children."

"Isn't he a good-looking dog?"

"Yes, he is, but he's all yours to care for. I have three children that take all my time."

That evening it was necessary to feed the dog, and the question came up as to what to feed him. The previous owner had told me what the dog was accustomed to eating (I had waited until the need came before saying anything). Now the time to come. "He eats Pablum." I said the words as if anyone would know. I wasn't quite prepared for the full faced look, "PABLUM?"

In fairness I did recognize Pablum was not the ordinary. After mixing the Pablum and feeding the dog, I fixed a few bales of hay to form a shelter. His home was to be outdoors.

He made very little noise during the night, but was up early and ready for his breakfast.

By the time I got home from work the dog had been fed the scraps from lunch. After dinner, my wife scraped the dishes then walked to the door, called Dusty, and gave him the scraps. After about a week in which she fed Dusty three times a day, I asked—

"Why are you feeding the dog? You said you wouldn't feed him or care for him."
"Someone has to care for your dog."

"Well, if you didn't beat me to the job, I take care of him."

"And when you are not at home?"

This was the way it started. In the years that followed, things never changed. The wife took over the feeding of Dusty. They became good friends.

The children took over the training of the dog and made him a member of the family. He accepted the position. Not only did he accept the position, but adopted the attitude of equality.

Before I get too far ahead of myself, let's back up to milking time – Dusty's second day at his new home. I took my milk bucket, called the dog, and headed to the barn. The cow saw us coming, and started for the barn also. We put the grain for the cow, in the manger just in time to step back and let the cow pass. Being of the nature she was, she took an extra step in passing to step on the dog. Dusty yelped. I snapped the stanchion closed and picked up Dusty. He seemed to be all right. I washed the cow's udder and began milking.

Whether she understood it or not, I explained some of the facts of life to the cow, pointing out some of the pitfalls she could encounter in passing through this life- especially if she persisted in being obnoxious around Dusty. I'll give Dusty credit- he learned fast. That hulk of a cow never had another chance to step on him.

The city began to grow up around us. The population increased and the novelty of the farm animals began to attract children from all around.

One afternoon, as I drove into the yard there seemed to be more children on hand than usual. I express the idea to my wife but she put me straight.
"It's a normal day, I generally have about 26 kids all day long."

"Every day?"

"Yes, this is normal."

You can call that normal if you choose, but not I. Life had changed at our place. My sweet wife was worn out at the end of the day tending too many children. I went outside and told the children to go home. They told me their mother had told them not to come back until they were called. The wife told me that their lunches were put out for them at noon, and the door was locked. The wife further explained the new order of things while I strove for understanding.

After thinking things over, the answer was obvious; we had to move.

Without too much trouble I found a piece of ground about 15 miles southwest from where we lived. I packed the family in the car. And took them to see the new home.

Dusty was becoming a large dog. His shoulder was as high as my knee. Winter was coming fast. We built a small house for his temporary shelter. Dusty was still an outside dog. The cold weather and nature put a most striking coat on Dusty through the winter, it was thick and shiny. It was not unusual to see Dusty curled up in the snow with the cat curled on top of him.

Dusty was always a ready playmate for the kids. He could duck a snowball with great ability. He never learned to retaliate, but never avoided a snowball fight. He could do many of the things the children did, and he was always present and participating to the fullest extent possible. When we were feeding the cattle, Dusty would "entertain" the cow by teasing them through the fence. Dusty liked to torment Star in particular. I don't believe he ever forgot her first attempt to shorten in his life. When there was nothing more interesting to do, he would take a few minutes to let her know he was alive and well.

Would you believe Dusty knew how to play 'fox and geese'? When playing the game with the children he never cheated, he followed the path made by the children.

When I milked, Dusty would come into the barn and wait for his warm milk. You might say he was spoiled, but he loved warm milk morning and night. He always left the barn before I turned the cow loose. When he teased her he would always have a barrier between the two of them. He never allowed a direct confrontation. He always kept me or one of the boys, or a fence between Star and himself.

I don't believe he was afraid of her. I believe it was not his nature to be stirring up trouble.

By spring, Dusty had learned another little stunt. He would greet me as I got out of the car and as we walked to the house, he would reach down and untie my shoes. Why did he do that? You figure it out. Before I'm through with this story he will have much more to wonder about.

You know how curious relatives are when one of the family moves. The rest of the family comes to the new house to see how well you did. On this particular day one of the wife's sisters came to see how things were, and she brought her little toddler with her. While they stood at the door, Dusty came over to see the strangers. The little boy was checking Dusty's tonsils when the mother looked around and saw the little boy's arm in the dog's mouth. She started to panic when I told her to relax, the dog would be happier than she when the little boy removed his arm. When the arm was removed, Dusty backed off far enough to avoid a similar incident.

Dusty was very aware of the difference in the sizes of children.

An example of Dusty's distinguishing of size was displayed in his playing the games with the kids. The game of tag was played by all the children at the same time; large and small. You've played the game, you decide who is "it" and then that one must touch someone to pass "it" on. Dusty would not be left out of any game if it were possible for him to play. When he was "it" he would catch the child he was after, and placed two front paws on their back.

The small children would receive a very light tag, while the larger boys would receive his full weight between the shoulders, sometimes toppling them. Now this was not Dusty's idea. The boys were not very careful when they tagged Dusty. They all took their tumbles with good humor.

To give you an idea of Dusty's sense of humor: Dusty would meet me when I drove into the yard and walked to the house with me. We would talk things over on the way. I did the talking and he listened. Somewhere between the car and the house, he would bump my leg at the right time to hook my toe behind my other foot causing me to stumble. Dusty would continue to trot ahead knowing all the rest of the story.

Dusty kept his eyes on the kids. One spring morning we were planting raspberry starts; our newest, Nancy, was toddling around in her snowsuit. We had one row planted and were halfway finished with the second row, when Dusty barked. The wife became alarmed and looked for Nancy.

"Look in the ditch!"

Elaine, 10 years old, ran to the ditch. Her terrible scream left no doubt as to the thoughts in her mind. In a bound, I was at the ditch side reaching for Nancy. She was floating on her back about 3 inches underwater. The chill of the water made her hold her breath. The fact is she had taken no water, and suffered no ill effects. It left us with a great deal of gratitude toward the dog who by this act had probably saved the life of our little girl.

A few months later the same little girl decided to join the big boys in the pasture. She made her way through the fence and into the field. She was well into the pasture when the old black cow saw her. The boys caught sight of Nancy about the same time. Knowing the disposition of the cow, the boys broke into a sudden sprint in an effort to reach Nancy before the cow. It was a hopeless try, but one of those things you do automatically.

The cow had the race in the bag, closing fast when a blur of fur passed Nancy in the direction of the cow. About 20 feet past the child, Dusty sunk his teeth into the cow's tender nose and let his body swing. The 70 odd pound of dog swinging to the side and the cow's neck back and around so the cow was thrown off balance. Between 1300 and 1400 pounds of beef hit the ground with a thud. By the time the dazed bovine recovered her wits, the boys were on the scene, the toddler was out of danger, and on her way to the house.

One of the games the children like to play in the summer was to go on a safari to the wash just west of the farm. The object of this safari was to capture the wild and wily gray squirrel. Regardless of what you may think, the squirrel can be captured by sub teenage children. One of the best tools to take along on a squirrel safari is a large collie dog. In the scramble for the elusive rodent, if he's willing, the dog may just place his foot on the gray ball of fur until one of the hunters can manage to get the wild beast into the cage. The cage -- a cardboard box, of course. Some of the character traits of the dog, Dusty, was the fact he never felt the least degree inferior to people, other animals, or anything. On the other hand, there was never, ever an air of superiority. There was always an air of respect for others and for himself.

I have to tell you an experience the wife related to me. As you know, the farm where we lived was near the "end of the earth." This was a quote from one of our close relatives who lived near the city all his life. With these thoughts in the back of her mind, the wife was feeling a little depressed one fall day. The two older children were in school. The third child, a boy, was on his daily walk around the fence line of the farm. This walk was always in the company of Dusty. They were good friends. So with his arm over the dog's shoulder the daily walk was in progress. The wife, watching from the window, could see the white hair just over the top of the grain, and later, the alfalfa.

Mother thought she could hear the boy crying. Why had she permitted his father to bring the children and herself so far from civilization? Her depression deepened. As his voice came nearer, she gradually realized the lad was not crying, but singing.

When he reached the temporary home we had built, he came to his mother and with all the joy he could crowd into his small voice he said, "Thanks, Mama, for moving to the farm." It was the wife's last feeling of depression for having left the comforts of the suburb living.

If I haven't given you the idea that Dusty was a handsome dog, I will tell you one more time, he was. I believe this was the cause of what developed into a tragedy. We had been away for the afternoon and when we returned there was no Dusty to welcome us. We thought this was so unusual we made several comments about where he could be? Could it be a girlfriend? Well, he will be home in the morning. Morning came, but Dusty was not there ready for the milking, Dusty never ever missed milking.

The days went by one after another and Dusty never returned. Had he been stolen? Run over by a car? Shot, poisoned, torn to bits by huge animal? The thoughts that run through a person's mind, triggered by apprehension, can be devastating. Day after day went by, then week after week, all hope had gone. Dusty was a beautiful memory.

One bright morning just before lunch, one of the children noticed a tramp dog coming slowly up the road. (People were always dumping unwanted dogs and cats.) As he came closer we noticed his limp and terrible fatigue. Dusty? Could it be? I had heard the expression "a rat, a bone, hank of hair," now I have seen the reason for its coining.

We doctored his feet, they were raw and caked with blood. His coat was dull and had the appearance of rags. His flesh was nearly a thing of the past. It took several weeks to rebuild his body. Fresh warm milk morning and night, tons of tender loving care from the whole family.

Aside from the incident of his disappearance, Dusty lived a very pleasant and useful life. It was a comfort to have him on watch outside at night. I can't explain exactly how Dusty was able to convey meaning with a bark, but even when I was asleep he could bark a single bark or two, I would wake, slip on clothing while commenting to my wife, "the cows are out" or "someone has turned the water in on us." Maybe was a chicken, turkey, or some other minor problem but it was out. It was nice to have the warrant before things got out of hand.

On the spring day when Dusty had passed his 9th birthday, we brought three wiener pigs from a neighbor. They grew well for about two weeks, then they rapidly grew sick. The first pig died in a day and a half. The next two pigs followed the first the next day. The veterinarian said they had a familiar malady, but I had been associated with animals long enough to know his guess was in error. In any case it was too fast moving to be anything about. Because of my doubts I determined to burn the pigpen, pigs, and all associated.

We counted the loss to be unfortunate, and dismissed the incident.
Our number two son had a paper route, and the neighbor who had sold the pigs to us was one of his customers. The man came to the road and stopping the boy asking about the welfare of the wieners he had sold us. The boy indicated they had all died. The man told the boy the whole litter, including the mother had also died, he told my son the cause of the death and that we should burn their pen and all that they might have had any contact with. The neighbor called and said that as soon as he could, he would replace the diseased pigs in order to make things right. The event that we did not anticipate was that Dusty would contract the disease. Well, he did, and there was nothing we could do about it.

(94) The Dog
By: Theo John Nielsen - 1980
Transcribed by Jeffrey Evans

He was the biggest of the litter.

His feeding schedule was anytime food was available; milk from his mother and Pablum from the owner.

His price was $35.00 without papers, and he was on his way to a new home. He missed his brothers and sisters, but the warm fresh milk morning and night helped him to forget; besides the milk there were scraps from the table three times a day.

The lady of the house said, "What do we need a dog for?"

The master's brilliant reply was, "The kids need a dog."

"I won't feed him; he's your dog and your chore."

"Okay."

So I became the chore of the master. At 6:00 a.m. every morning and at 6:00 p.m. every evening the master and I would walk to the barn to milk the cow.

I remember our first trips to the barn tonight of my arrival at the new home.

We walked the path worn in the dirt by many such trips. The master carried an empty bucket. When we stepped inside the barn we removed the lid from a huge 50 gallon drum and dipped grain for the cow.

As we approached the manger from the cow side she came trotting into the barn. I had never seen so large an animal.

She was at least ten times my height. Apprehension gripped me as she approached; the earth shook beneath her great feet.

As she came to where the master and I stood she made a clever sidestep, hitting me a glancing and painful blow.

My body screamed with pain and my heart filled with hate. The young people loved me, the master was proud of me, the mistress tolerated me and the cow wanted me dead. Life would surely be interesting.

Sometime in the next year we moved to a new home. The reason the master gave was the mistress was the neighborhood babysitter. (The area had been building rapidly). During this year the mistress had taken over the "chore" of feeding me. She said it was because the job was left to her and she couldn't see me starve.

I had my own idea about her reasons. The way she petted my head and brushed my coat with her hand said there was more. The most convincing thing she did was the way she talked to me. Her voice was soft and rich. Its deep kindness was very soothing -- I kept all her thoughts confidential.

At the new home, things were not easy. As it turned out there was no water on the place, nor was there any electricity. The house was small, but "temporary". The size of the house or the other conveniences was not important to me. I was never allowed in the house and there always seem to be enough to eat.

The mistress talk to me about these things and sometimes she seemed a little bitter or greatly disappointed. There was often a tear in her eye.

Two of the children were in school -- a boy, the eldest and a girl, a grade younger. The next smaller person was a boy he was a little taller than I so we saw things almost eye to eye.

Every day in that beautiful fall weather we would walk the fence line of our farm. The round trip would take more than an hour and take us about one quarter of a mile from the house.

The boy would put his arm over my shoulder and we would start walking. I never did understand all the curiosity that child could exhibit over the most unimportant things, bugs, rocks, dirt, posts, weeds, flowers and on and on.

He would tell me the most unbelievable stories about their things and sometimes he would sing. You should hear that lad sing. On a quiet day the still air would carry his voice to the house and beyond.

On one such day, my young friend sang and sang. There were frequent stops along the way and the last leg of the trip was made in haste, as if we were in a hurry to return to the house.

When we came close to the house the mistress came to meet us, all teary-eyed. My walking companion burst in a run and said "Oh, Mama, aren't you glad we live here?" Mama seemed a little puzzled. Had she misinterpreted the sounds my little friend had made?

I really don't know, what people think but I never saw a tear in her eye after that day. Well, almost never, but I'll tell you about that later.

The winter passed. My coat was thick and shiny. Thanks to my breeding and feeding I was larger than most of my kind! In some ways I was like my master; large, strong, and maybe a little too proud. Who knows?

Spring! How busy can a family be? Work early! Work late! What tireless people! Would you believe, using your silver haired children as markers in the dark so you might work just a little longer?

I will say this: whatever they did they did together! Yes, they did play. They ever had a way of playing while they worked. I don't understand what I just said, but that was how it seemed to me.

Now, I just have to tell about a little Safari we went on one day. We did this quite often, the kids and me. Well, just a little west of our farm there was a gully with brush and sticks and lots of other things. Among the other things was what they called squirrels, little animals with big bushy tails.

It was their ambition to catch the little frizzy animals, but they had never succeeded. It was against my better judgment but all that squealing and excitement got to me so I pitched in. I had my foot on the back of one and waited for the kids to take it from me.

The oldest girl was first to me. You may not believe this, but after she got to me she didn't want to take it. She would put her hand down close and then pull it back. The biggest boy, now 8 years old, said he wasn't afraid, "Stand back".

Well sir. Before he could think, that little girl had reached down, grabbed that squirrel, dropped it and had her torn finger in her mouth. The Safari had come to an abrupt end and the little girl was on the road to the doctor's office for a shot. Would you believe we never tried to catch squirrels again?

Another thing happened that summer. I taught the children a new game. We called it tag. It's where you touch someone and then run saying, "you're it." Maybe you have played a similar game but I doubt if you played it the way we did.

I would be sitting watching the kids at play when one of the boys would tackle me knocking me to the ground. They would then 'cuff' me and run off with a "you're it".

We had played a lot of rough house but this was new wrinkle. On impulse I ran after him and leaped striking him between the shoulder blades and sending him nose first in the grass.

If I thought that would put an end to the game I was mistaken. He was up in a flash and headed straight for me. That's how it began. It never ended it just expanded to include all the children large and small.

I wouldn't want you to suppose I treated them all the same. The little ones I nudged very gently and the big ones got back what they gave. It was great fun.

We built a big, fine, house in front of the small one and I would spend time lying on the front porch watching the cars go by. They were not a great many cars but some of them would slow down and look at our house. Sometimes I had the feeling they were looking at me.

One day that feeling proved to be true. Before this unsuspecting soul could figure it out I was tied in the back of the pickup truck speeding down the road.

Things were never quite clear to me at this point. I was surprised and so bewildered, I had no idea about we were going; nor even which direction. One thing I did know, I was frightened and near panic.

I don't know how long we traveled or how fast we were going. Darkness came and I watched the stars come out. The side I laid on ached. I wanted to be in natural position but it was useless to try.

Finally it was over and I was put into a fenced area, small and tall. A few leaps proved the uselessness of trying to jump over the fence. The ground was covered with cement, it was hopeless.

The next day passed with no visitors until after dark. I was given of bowl of what was said to be the best "dog food".

Have you tasted "dog food"? I never had after all, what's wrong with potatoes and gravy and meet scraps? What's wrong with homemade bread and homemade butter? "Dog food!!!" Yuck!

By the third day, I was hungry. I was homesick. I was without hope.
As I lay brooding over my plight a young man about 16 years of age came toward my pen. I lay very quietly watching as he drew near; wondering what was in store for me now.

He lifted the latch on the gate and pulled the gate toward him so as to make a small crack. Quick as a flash I put my nose to his, bowling over him and I was free. Oh how I ran!

I ran through fields, over lawns, across streets until my lungs wanted to burst. When weariness forced me to stop I found a large bush in which to hide. It was cool there and soon my breathing became normal. I was far enough from the "pen" that I'm sure the people had given up looking for me. On the other hand it wasn't worth taking a chance. I must be very careful.

I had to find a home but the only thing I had going for me was a sort of "gut" feeling, maybe "hunch" is a better word. Whatever the feeling was, it was all I had, so off I went.

I traveled at night and hid by day. I raided a garbage can. It wasn't much and it wasn't good, but I was growing weak.

The days grew into weeks and I changed my plans, Caution was abandoned and I traveled almost 24 hours a day. The houses and barns looked familiar now. I wanted to break into a run but I didn't have the strength.

Would the miles ever pass?!

I was just a block from home when one of the children cried "Dusty!" I don't know who it was that called my name, all I know is that I was weary beyond belief.

We all walked the last block together, the chatter was incessant and scrambled, but oh, so good to hear.

First, I was fed, but not too much. Then the master went over every inch of me looking for anything that might need attention. He washed my bleeding feet and put some cool salve on them. Food and rest would make me better, he said. The children were very sympathetic and very helpful. I never lacked for snacks.

Have you ever been taken for granted? The method I used to get my share of attention from the master was to walk along by his side and undo his shoe laces.

This worked sometimes and when it didn't I invented another way. When the master was walking toward the house I trotted alongside and at the right moment, bumped his legs so as to knock the toe behind the other heel, causing him to stumble.

"You no good dog! Where did you learn that trick?"

Then I would get my ears scratched –heaven --my side thumped and my head rubbed.

He would sit on the steps petting my head and talk to me as an equal. Then "I've got work to do 'useless', see you later."

I was a success.

The following summer I became a hero, or so the boys said. It happened this way… The Master's 8th child was a girl and just learning to walk well. Well enough that is, to find a hole is in the corral fence and crawl through. She walked through the corral and into the pasture where my arch enemy reigned.

Over the years that cow and I had cultivated our dislikes for one another in every way we could think of. I'll admit I provoked her at every opportunity. Some of the opportunities I made myself.

Back to my story. The boys were at the far end of the pasture, the cow about midway in the pasture and little Nancy was headed straight for trouble.

At this point in time there were three people who could handle that ill-tempered cow -- the two boys and the master.

The cow and I had never had a head-on confrontation. I didn't want one now or ever. As things were developing at this moment I could see my time had run out. There was no way around this one.

That cow had spotted the toddler coming toward her, and being the opportunist she was, saw another chance to do injury to a helpless, unsuspecting being.

The boys saw the imminent disaster and called to Nancy to go back. They were too far away to help. They were straining every muscle, but in vain.

Nancy didn't understand the danger, but even if she had it was too late now.

I had made my decision and was running at break-neck speed toward the cow. I passed Nancy and in two more leaps had sunk my fangs deep into her tender nose. As I did so my momentum snapped; my 80 pounds, in an arc struck the cow's side. Her tender nose was pulled around to the side caused her to lose balance and she fell on her back with a heavy thump.

When the cow had regained her breath and her senses (if she ever had any), we, the victors, were leaving the field of battle. I never got weary of hearing the boys tell the tale.

This next incident should prove to the most skeptical, the fact that people have feelings just as dogs do.

The master had gotten some wiener pigs from the neighbor before the week was over the three of them had died in a strange and gruesome manner.

When the first one died, the master removed it from the pen and tossed its body far from the others to prevent them from getting the disease if they didn't already have it.

Curiosity led me to close examination of the corpse but I was no smarter than before. It just didn't make sense.

Be that as it may, they were dead! Apparently, from something very contagious. The master put the dead pigs into the pen with everything they could have touched and set it afire. He hoped by this act, to eliminate the disease from the farm.

He might have been successful if I had not been so nosey. You guessed right, I had caught the disease and was running a fever. Shots of penicillin did no good. The master looked down at me with clenched jaw

"What can I do for you, Dusty?"

I didn't know. All I could do was look my shame and apologies to my family. Maybe sometime in the future they would be able to forgive me for bringing sorrow to their lives.

I was permitted to linger in the spirit until the burial was over. The boys made sure I wasn't cramped in the grave. Gently the loose earth filled the grave and they had done all that could be done for me. I had lived a very rich 9 years. I could ask for no more.

(95) Lost

While waiting for the stage presentation to resume, someone came out and made an appeal for help for a children's program. I was touched by the need for personal service that was made, and I went to the place where the man had directed. Either the directions were incomplete or misunderstood, for I didn't find my objective.

The biggest problem I discovered was that I was uncertain as to where I had left my family. I searched in several auditoriums that by now were empty. After much time and frustration, I located the music hall for which I had been searching. Of course, it was empty also. Since we were from out of town, the next question was. Where did they go? My wife is physically handicapped, so there is another factor in the puzzle.

I thought about the home where she was reared, and then remembered it had been torn down. She could have gone to one of the children's homes. Which was the most likely? Of course the ones she was with. Phone numbers, can't remember. Some of the others would know. Where is a phone?

The search for a telephone in the middle of the night is a "night-mare". Frustration and fatigue took their toll, and after too much time I decided to take a cab to a known child's home. Finally stopped a cab and the man said, "Where to?" I suppose I was so tired, I was unable to think. The cabbie pulled over and said, "Well?" It didn't help. I pulled out my wallet and it was no help. "What's this?" the man said. I had a small book in my pocket. In it were names and phone numbers of a few persons. He knew where there was a phone and dialed until he had a response. He drove me to my daughter's house, collected his fee, and was I ever relieved.

A good night's sleep is always welcome, even when it runs into the next morning. My daughter acted like late breakfasts were a routine happening at her house. The family always treat us with love.

We were able to notify the wife of my where-abouts so that she wouldn't worry all night, but it was time I rejoined her. My hat and sports jacket, and I was off for another daughter's home. The breeze was coming up making the air feel fresher. I fumbled for my car keys then glanced around for the car. There were several cars in the driveway, but not mine.

I suppose one of the children had dropped me here, and that my car was at the other house. I stepped back into the house, and announced I would need a lift to the other place. Several of the grandchildren volunteered. We were off. Our arrival was welcomed, and all were assured everything was all right.

An hour's visit and I thought it was time to return home. We gathered our belongings and I pushed the wife towards the door. Out on the side walk she said, "Where's the car?" I was a little befuddled when I couldn't see it setting there. I thought, but I didn't have a ready answer. I know I hadn't come in my car, but then who might have it?

"You drove it to the concert last night, Dad." That's it, it's uptown. "Well I suppose it's in the parking lot. Can someone take us there? We'll go home from there." This complicated things for some of the kids, but it would work out.

The car was as we suspected, waiting for us in the lot just as we had left it.

With the wife comfortably seated we were on our way home. It was several miles home, so I determined to use the freeway. I pulled onto the southbound ramp, brought up my speed and merged. "Why are we going this way?" My wife was looking at me with questions in her eyes, as well as in her tone. "Going home." I replied. "We haven't lived in this direction for more than three years." Now there seems to be a problem, if we don't live in this direction, where do we live? "Well I guess we'll just have to get off the freeway and start over." I took the next off ramp, and was back on again as quick as I could make two left turns.

"Is this better?"

"I should hope so," She was content.

"Suppose you tell me directions until we get home." I thought this would get me off the "hook" until I could sort this whole thing out.

"Just stay on the freeway for the next four hours." It's what she actually said.

This did not help my sorting process.

We stopped for lunch at a little place I like to eat. I could not find same. We settled for a hamburger, fast food, and were on our way again.

My idea to sort things out as we drove worked very well. The landscape, the roads, the skyline all became familiar, and we were "home free," as they say.

As I have thought about the above experience the past few days, a thought has occurred to me that I have not the willingness to explore.

The possibility of. . . I'm not even going to say the word.

Life goes on for us, and the experience spoken of seems further away every day. Bad food, fatigue, no matter, but it was a frightening time.

"Honey, John wants me to work in his shop for a few days next week." John had just called with a problem that I could relieve.

"Okay, I'll be ready. When do you want to go?"

Riding that many hours was very painful to my wife, but she was afraid I'd get sleepy while driving.

"We could see Christie's new baby while we are there."

I thought this might take some of the hurt out of the idea.

"We'll go about nine or so."

Next morning we packed everything we would need, checking for the things we always forget. Wheeling her to the car, she remembered water to bring on the road. With that on board, we were on our way.

Mid seventies, and a bad back are no fun on the road for four hours, but Honey likes me, and wants to be with me, and I like that.

Cars, cars, cars, everywhere. I'm doing seventy, but you'd think I was standing still. I'm sure glad I don't live in the big city.

"Where do you want to get off the freeway?" We hadn't talked about where we were staying.

"Let's go to Johns." We won't have to move from there until we go home." She was right.

We had a very pleasant evening. Our social interchange as always was exigent. The children are always wanting to get us a drink, or some other comfort. I am very pleased with the quality of our grandchildren's upbringing.

My wife sat on the edge of the bed while I removed her shoes and stockings. It was a good bed, but not my water bed.

Have you ever awakened in a strange room, and wondered where you were? So have I. In a few seconds things come to an understanding, and we are oriented. Not today. Yes, this is my wife. This is not my bed. This is not my house. I can wake someone with enough noise, but that would give the whole secret away.

www.ingramcontent.com/pod-product-compliance
Lightning Source LLC
Chambersburg PA
CBHW042008150426
43195CB00002B/56